BIRDS OF
COASTAL
BRITISH
COLUMBIA
and the Pacific Northwest Coast

D0967866

by Nancy Baron & John Acorn

The Publisher: Lone Pine Publishing

10145 - 81 Ave.	1808 B Street NW, Suite 140
Edmonton, AB T6E 1W9	Auburn, WA 98001
Canada	USA

Website: www.lonepinepublishing.com

Canadian Cataloguing in Publication Data

Birds of Coastal British Columbia

Includes bibliographical references and index.
Published also as: Birds of the Pacific Northwest Coast
ISBN 1-55105-098-6

1. Birds—British Columbia—Pacific Coast—Identification. 2. Birds—Pacific Coast (U.S.)—Identification. 3. Birds—British Columbia—Pacific Coast—Handbooks, manuals, etc. 4. Birds—Pacific Coast (U.S.)—Handbooks, manuals, etc. I. Acorn, John Harrison, 1958- II. Title. III. Title: Birds of Coastal British Columbia

QL685.5.B7B37 1997   598'.09711'1   C97–910580–3

Senior Editor: Nancy Foulds
Editorial: Roland Lines, Edrea Daniel
Production Manager: David Dodge
Design and Layout: Michelle Bynoe, Gregory Brown
Cover Design: Jun Lee
Cover Illustration: Gary Ross
Technical Review: Richard Cannings
Separations and Film: Elite Lithographers Co. Ltd., Edmonton, AB, Canada
Printing: Friesens Corporation
Cartographer: Volker Bodegom
Illustrations: Ted Nordhagen, Gary Ross, Ewa Pluciennik

The publisher gratefully acknowledges the support of Alberta Community Development and the Department of Canadian Heritage.

Contents

ACKNOWLEDGMENTS

Many individuals were of great help to us during the writing of this book, and their contributions are much appreciated: Mandy Fisher, Chris Fisher, Johnny Mikes, David Stirling, Glenn Rollans, Russell Rogers and Dena Stockburger. As well, Dick Cannings deserves special mention and thanks for the time and effort he put into reading and reviewing the draft manuscript. The book owes its final form to discussions with Shane Kennedy and Nancy Foulds, as well as the efforts of Edrea Daniel, Roland Lines, David Dodge, Gregory Brown, Michelle Bynoe, Carol Dragich and Jun Lee. Finally, we are grateful for the superb artwork created for this project by Gary Ross and Ted Nordhagen, and we feel privileged to have their work appear alongside our words.

A QUICK KEY TO THE BIRDS

This complete illustrated key to the birds contained in this book can be used to identify the birds quickly.

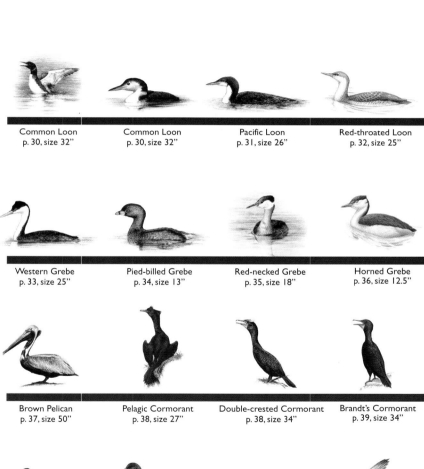

Common Loon
p. 30, size 32"

Common Loon
p. 30, size 32"

Pacific Loon
p. 31, size 26"

Red-throated Loon
p. 32, size 25"

Western Grebe
p. 33, size 25"

Pied-billed Grebe
p. 34, size 13"

Red-necked Grebe
p. 35, size 18"

Horned Grebe
p. 36, size 12.5"

Brown Pelican
p. 37, size 50"

Pelagic Cormorant
p. 38, size 27"

Double-crested Cormorant
p. 38, size 34"

Brandt's Cormorant
p. 39, size 34"

Black-footed Albatross
p. 40, size 36"

Northern Fulmar
p. 41, size 18"

Sooty Shearwater
p. 42, size 19"

Fork-tailed Storm-Petrel
p. 43, size 8"

SEABIRDS

GULL-LIKE BIRDS

Common Murre
p. 44, size 17"

Pigeon Guillemot
p. 45, size 13"

Tufted Puffin
p. 46, size 15"

Rhinoceros Auklet
p. 47, size 15"

Marbled Murrelet
p. 48, size 9.5"

Ancient Murrelet
p. 48, size 9.5"

Cassin's Auklet
p. 49, size 9.5"

Parasitic Jaeger
p. 50, size 19"

Heermann's Gull
p. 51, size 19"

Glaucous-winged Gull
p. 52, size 26"

Western Gull
p. 53, size 26"

Herring Gull
p. 54, size 26"

Thayer's Gull
p. 55, size 23"

California Gull
p. 56, size 20"

Ring-billed Gull
p. 57, size 19"

Mew Gull
p. 57, size 18"

Bonaparte's Gull
p. 58, size 13"

Bonaparte's Gull
p. 59, size 13"

Caspian Tern
p. 60, size 21"

Common Tern
p. 61, size 15"

Trumpeter Swan p. 62, size 60"	Tundra Swan p. 63, size 53"	Mute Swan p. 63 size 60"	Canada Goose p. 64, size 25-43"

Snow Goose
p. 65, size 28"

Brant
p. 66, size 24"

Mallard
p. 67, size 25"

Northern Shoveler
p. 68, size 20"

Gadwall
p. 69, size 21"

Northern Pintail
p. 70, size 26"

American Wigeon
p. 71, size 24"

Green-winged Teal
p. 72, size 15-16"

Blue-winged Teal
p. 72, size 15-16"

Cinnamon Teal
p. 73, size 15-16"

Surf Scoter
p. 74, size 20"

White-winged Scoter
p. 75, size 20"

Black Scoter
p. 75, size 20"

Harlequin Duck
p. 76, size 18"

Oldsquaw
p. 77, size 18"

Greater Scaup
p. 78, size 20"

WATERFOWL

Lesser Scaup
p. 79, size 17"

Ring-necked Duck
p. 79, size 17"

Canvasback
p. 80, size 20"

Bufflehead
p. 81, size 13"

Barrow's Goldeneye
p. 82, size 18"

Common Goldeneye
p. 83, size 18"

Ruddy Duck
p. 84, size 15"

Wood Duck
p. 85, size 18"

Common Merganser
p. 86, size 25"

Red-breasted Merganser
p. 87, size 23"

Hooded Merganser
p. 88, size 18"

American Coot
p. 89, size 15"

WADING BIRDS

Great Blue Heron
p. 90, size 46"

American Bittern
p. 91, size 23"

Green Heron
p. 92, size 17"

Sandhill Crane
p. 93, size 41"

Virginia Rail
p. 94, size 9"

Sora
p. 95, size 8"

Black Oystercatcher
p. 96, size 17"

Black-bellied Plover
p. 97, size 11"

Killdeer
p. 98, size 10"

Common Snipe
p. 99, size 11"

Greater Yellowlegs
p. 100, size 14"

Lesser Yellowlegs
p. 100, size 10"

Solitary Sandpiper
p. 101, size 8"

Red-necked Phalarope
p. 102, size 8"

Wilson's Phalarope
p. 103, size 8"

Short-billed Dowitcher
p. 104, size 11"

Western Sandpiper
p. 105, size 6"

Least Sandpiper
p. 106, size 5"

Semipalmated Sandpiper
p. 107, size 6"

Sanderling
p. 108, size 8"

Dunlin
p. 109, size 8"

Pectoral Sandpiper
p. 110, size 8.5"

Spotted Sandpiper
p. 111, size 7.5"

Surfbird
p. 112, size 10"

Red Knot
p. 113, size 10.5"

Black Turnstone
p. 114, size 9"

GROUSE-LIKE BIRDS

BIRDS OF PREY

Wandering Tattler
p. 115, size 11.5"

Whimbrel
p. 116, size 17"

Ring-necked Pheasant
p. 117, size M-33", F-21"

Ruffed Grouse
p. 118, size 16"

Blue Grouse
p. 119, size 20"

White-tailed Ptarmigan
p. 120, size 12"

California Quail
p. 121, size 10"

Turkey Vulture
p. 122, size 27"

Northern Harrier
p. 123, size 18"

Northern Goshawk
p. 124, size 21"

Cooper's Hawk
p. 125, size 16"

Sharp-shinned Hawk
p. 125, size 11"

Red-tailed Hawk
p. 126, size 22"

Rough-legged Hawk
p. 127, size 22"

Bald Eagle
p. 128, size 35"

Osprey
p. 129, size 24"

Merlin
p. 130, size 12"

American Kestrel
p. 131, size 10.5"

Peregrine Falcon
p. 132, size 18"

Great Horned Owl
p. 133, size 22"

Snowy Owl
p. 134, size 23"

Barn Owl
p. 135, size 16"

Barred Owl
p. 136, size 21"

Spotted Owl
p. 137, size 17"

Northern Saw-whet Owl
p. 138, size 8"

Western Screech-Owl
p. 139, size 8"

Northern Pygmy-Owl
p. 139, size 7"

Short-eared Owl
p. 140, size 15"

Belted Kingfisher
p. 141, size 13"

Rock Dove
p. 142, size 12"

Band-tailed Pigeon
p. 143, size 15"

Mourning Dove
p. 143, size 12"

Common Nighthawk
p. 144, size 9"

Rufous Hummingbird
p. 145, size 3.5"

Anna's Hummingbird
p. 146 size 3.5"

Vaux's Swift
p. 147, size 4.5"

Barn Swallow
p. 148, size 6.75"

Cliff Swallow
p. 149, size 5.5"

Tree Swallow
p. 150, size 5.5"

Violet-green Swallow
p. 150, size 5.5"

Northern Rough-winged
Swallow
p. 151, size 5.5"

Hairy Woodpecker
p. 152, size 9.5"

Downy Woodpecker
p. 153, size 6.5"

Red-breasted Sapsucker
p. 154, size 8"

Northern Flicker
p. 155, size 12"

Lewis' Woodpecker
p. 156, size 10.5"

Pileated Woodpecker
p. 157, size 16"

Eastern Kingbird
p. 158, size 8"

Western Kingbird
p. 158, size 8"

Olive-sided Flycatcher
p. 159, size 7"

Western Wood-Pewee
p. 159, size 6"

Pacific-slope Flycatcher
p. 160, size 5.5"

Hammond's Flycatcher
p. 161, size 5.5"

Willow Flycatcher
p. 161, size 5.5"

Horned Lark
p. 162, size 8"

Sky Lark
p. 163, size 7"

American Pipit
p. 164, size 6"

Winter Wren
p. 165, size 4"

House Wren
p. 166, size 4.5"

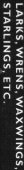

Bewick's Wren
p. 167, size 5.5"

Marsh Wren
p. 168, size 5"

American Dipper
p. 169, size 7"

Golden-crowned Kinglet
p. 170, size 3.5"

Ruby-crowned Kinglet
p. 171, size 4"

Gray Catbird
p. 172, size 9"

Northern Shrike
p. 173, size 10"

Cedar Waxwing
p. 174, size 7"

European Starling
p. 175, size 8"

Northwestern Crow
p. 176, size 16"

Common Raven
p. 177, size 24"

Gray Jay
p. 178, size 11.5"

Steller's Jay
p. 179, size 12"

Clark's Nutcracker
p. 180, size 12"

Bushtit
p. 181, size 4.5"

Black-capped Chickadee
p. 182, size 5.5"

Mountain Chickadee
p. 182, size 5.5"

Chestnut-backed
Chickadee
p. 183, size 5.5"

Red-breasted Nuthatch
p. 184, size 4.5"

Brown Creeper
p. 185, size 5"

THRUSHES

American Robin
p. 186, size 9"

Varied Thrush
p. 187, size 10"

Swainson's Thrush
p. 188, size 7"

Hermit Thrush
p. 189, size 7"

VIREOS & WARBLERS

Red-eyed Vireo
p. 190, size 6"

Warbling Vireo
p. 191, size 5"

Solitary Vireo
p. 192, size 5"

Hutton's Vireo
p. 193, size 4.5"

Yellow-rumped Warbler
p. 194, size 6"

Orange-crowned Warbler
p. 195, size 5"

Yellow Warbler
p. 196, size 5"

Wilson's Warbler
p. 197, size 5"

MacGillivray's Warbler
p. 198, size 5"

Common Yellowthroat
p. 199, size 4.5"

Townsend's Warbler
p. 200, size 4"

Black-throated Gray
Warbler
p. 201, size 4"

BLACKBIRDS & TANAGERS

Red-winged Blackbird
p. 202, size 8"

Brewer's Blackbird
p. 203, size 9"

Brown-headed Cowbird
p. 204, size 7"

Western Meadowlark
p. 205, size 9"

Bullock's Oriole
p. 206, size 8"

Western Tanager
p. 207, size 7"

White-crowned Sparrow
p. 208, size 7.5"

Golden-crowned Sparrow
p. 209, size 7"

Fox Sparrow
p. 210, size 7.5"

Song Sparrow
p. 211, size 5"

Savannah Sparrow
p. 212, size 6"

Dark-eyed Junco
p. 213, size 6"

Spotted Towhee
p. 214, size 7"

Red Crossbill
p. 215, size 5.5"

House Finch
p. 216, size 6"

Purple Finch
p. 217, size 6"

Pine Siskin
p. 218, size 4.5"

American Goldfinch
p. 219, size 5"

Gray-crowned Rosy-Finch
p. 220, size 5.5"

Snow Bunting
p. 221, size 6"

Black-headed Grosbeak
p. 222, size 8"

Evening Grosbeak
p. 222, size 8"

Pine Grosbeak
p. 223, size 10"

House Sparrow
p. 224, size 6"

INTRODUCTION

THE JOYS OF BIRDWATCHING

Birdwatching has 'arrived' on the West Coast. Whether you pick up the binoculars a handful of times over the year or head out at every opportunity, you join an ever-increasing number of people who find the pursuit of birds one of the simplest and most rewarding means of spending time in the natural world.

But birdwatching, or 'birding,' as some prefer to call it, is challenging, and getting started is perhaps the hardest part. Thus, the intent of this book to help you get started. The standard North American field guides will also do the trick, but they can be daunting because they cover so many species over such a wide area. By focusing on the West Coast region alone, we hope to help you sort out your personal experiences with birds.

Telling birds apart at a glance requires more than a few hours spent with binoculars and a field guide. It could conceivably require a lifetime of careful study. After all, there are only a few birders in the Pacific Northwest who can identify all of our species with confidence, and almost everyone else finds they can get plenty of enjoyment from birding without necessarily 'mastering' it.

This book is intended to take you perhaps 80 percent of the way to becoming a skillful birder. That is to say, about 80 percent of the birds you see (individual birds, that is, not species of birds) will be relatively easy to identify with this book. Another 19 percent of the time, as a rough guess, you will see a familiar bird in an odd plumage, or bad light, and fail to recognize it. The final 1 percent of the time, you will be looking at a great rarity without realizing it. Sorry about that—it is that final 1 percent that gives 'avid' birders the ability to report exciting rarities so often. But let's not get ahead of ourselves!

The birds covered in this book can be found along the coasts of British Columbia and Washington, from the Coast Range and Cascades to the sea. We have also included Vancouver Island, the Gulf Islands, San Juan Islands and Queen Charlotte Islands in our coverage, and we have made a special effort to cover the birds most likely to be seen in and around the major cities.

BEGINNING TO LEARN THE BIRDS

The trick to becoming a competent birder is to know, at a glance, what general sort of bird you are looking at and then to know what the odds are of making such a sighting. In order to help you do that, we have first reduced the complete bird list by more or less ignoring most of the true rarities (called the 'accidentals' or 'vagrants' by ornithologists). Worry about these birds later since they have appeared in the Northwest Coast area only a handful of times. The remaining species have been dealt with either one at a time or grouped together when they are similar enough to warrant doing so.

To an ornithologist (a biologist who studies birds), the species is the fundamental unit of classification since the members of a species not only look alike but naturally interbreed with one another as well. Likewise, to a bird, the species is probably the only 'real' unit of classification, since another bird is either a member of the same species, in which case any number of important relationships might develop, or it is not. At least that is what happens most of the time. The boundaries between species are not always clear-cut, as in the case of Glaucous-winged and Western gulls, which keep to themselves in some places and interbreed extensively in others. Birdwatchers are sometimes frustrated when scientists 'lump' former species together or 'split' former species into new, separate species. However, the fuzziness of some species boundaries make consensus on such issues unlikely, since the accepted technical definition of a species is also continually being debated and, hopefully, refined.

Because the concept of species is so important to biologists, it has become important to birders as well. To most birders, a bird has not been identified unless it has been identified 'to species.' And yet most birders also use categories containing more than one species from time to time, as an aid to identification. You'll hear them say 'it's a peep,' or 'a dark phase buteo,' or 'one of the goldeneyes.' Hence the usefulness of occasional groupings.

In some cases in the text that follows, a treatment may contain one species—when that species is highly distinctive and unlikely to be confused with anything else. An example is the Belted Kingfisher. In other treatments, several species may be grouped together. One example is the dowitchers: medium-sized sandpipers that look, act and sound much the same and that can be distinguished from one another only with a great deal of practice. These groupings are intended as an aid to learning bird identification.

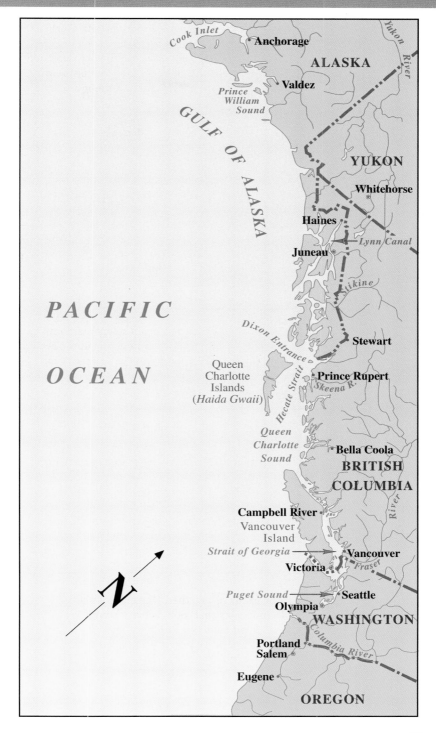

Of course, bird species can also be grouped together according to their evolutionary relationships, and this style is what scientifically oriented birdwatchers generally prefer. In ornithological circles, these groupings are—in order of increasing comprehensiveness—the genus, family and order, with many subgroupings in between. The birds are then arranged in a standard order that begins with those that are, in a general sense, most like the evolutionary ancestors of modern birds and ends with those that have been most strongly modified by evolutionary change.

To beginners, this order may not make much sense initally. But bird-watchers soon come to know that in all books of this sort, the back half will be devoted to songbirds (the 'passerines,' as they are formally known), and the front half begins with what could informally be called diving birds and seabirds, to be followed by gull-like birds, waterfowl, wading birds, shorebirds, grouse-like birds and birds of prey, then various birds that look more and more like true songbirds (everything from hummingbirds and doves to finch-like birds). In this book we have taken the standard order for birds and modified it slightly in order to group a greater number of similar birds together.

There is no simple way to arrange the diversity of bird life, since the evolution of birds was not a simple process. One thing is certain, however, and that is the fact that many readers will tell us we should have arranged the book alphabetically. Well, apart from placing similar, closely related birds far from one another in the text, this approach would soon prove impractical. For exam-ple, what if you saw a Merlin and decide to look it up alphabetically? Would you look under 'H' for hawk or 'F' for falcon? How about 'P' for it's former name, the Pigeon Hawk? All three would make sense, and none would be as simple as looking up the birds of prey, about a quarter of the way through the text, where they always are in books like this. There is really only one way to begin learning your birds and that is to bite the bullet, forget the shortcuts, and take pleasure in the task of actually identifying them.

THE TECHNIQUES OF BIRDWATCHING

Binoculars: As far as birding equipment goes, you will no doubt want to purchase a pair of binoculars, which can cost anywhere from $50 to $1500. The choices available are many. Most beginners pay less than $200 for their first pair, and many people are initially drawn to compact binoculars, which are small and lightweight. If you aren't that fussy about pin-sharp details on distant birds, this is a good way to begin.

If you are interested in the best image for the money, there are a few other things you should know. Binoculars come in two basic types: porro-prism (in which there is a distinct angular bend in the body of the binoculars) and roof-prism (in which the body is straight). Good quality porro-prism binoculars are less expensive than good quality roof-prism binoculars, and a first-rate pair of porros will cost about $300 to $400. Good roof-prism binoculars, which are often waterproof and nitrogen filled, can cost $800 or more. Expensive binoculars usually have better optics and are more ruggedly built, and they generally stand up far better to torture testing.

Binoculars, in general, are characterized by a two-number code. For example, a compact binocular might be an '8 x 21,' whereas a larger pair might have '7 x 40' stamped on it. In each case, the first number is the magnification of the binocular and the second number is the diameter, in millimeters, of the front lenses. Seven-power binoculars are easiest to hand hold and to find birds with; 10-power binoculars give a shakier but more detailed view. Larger lenses gather more light, and thus a 40 or 50 mm lens will perform much better at dusk than a 20 or 30 mm lens, at least at the same magnification. As well, some binoculars have a wider field of view than others, even if the two-number code seems identical, and this characteristic can be a very important factor. Many beginners have trouble finding birds in narrow-view binoculars. A good approach to finding birds is to lock your gaze on the subject and lift the binoculars right in front of your eyes. Don't take your eyes off the bird. Or you can search first for an obvious landmark near the bird (a bright flower or a dead branch, for example) and then find the bird from there.

For a beginner, an eight-power, porro-prism binocular with front lenses at least 35 mm in diameter would be a good, sensible place to start. One more word of advice: people can become strongly attached to their own pair of binoculars, no matter how inadequate they might be. When birding with other folks, if they don't mind, ask them to let you try their binoculars for comparison. Ask them what they like and don't like about them. You'll find that binocular preferences are largely a matter of personal taste. The only way to

21

know which model suits you best is to 'test drive' them and make your own judgment. Be forewarned, however, that as you come to appreciate good optics, your binocular budget is likely to expand. Once you've decided you really like birding, you'll probably want to invest in a pair of good binoculars.

Spotting Scopes and Cameras: A spotting scope (small telescope) and a tripod can also be helpful, especially for viewing distant waterfowl and shorebirds. Most spotting scopes are capable of at least 20-power magnification, making them useful for birds out of binocular range. Some will even allow you to take photographs through them, but you should know right now that the challenges of birdwatching pale in comparison to those encountered during bird photography.

If you are sincerely interested in bird photography, we recommend you purchase a 35 mm single-lens reflex camera with at least a 300 mm telephoto lens, and a good, solid tripod. Talk to a knowledgeable camera salesman, and be prepared to spend a lot of money. Your main challenge will be to obtain photos that are not blurred by camera shake or poor optics, but a good bird photo can be well worth the trouble and expense.

Birding by Ear: At some point you'll probably want to learn bird songs. The technique of birding by ear is gaining popularity because listening for birds can be more efficient than trying to see them. When experienced birders do breeding bird surveys each June in North America, they rely mostly on song recognition and very little on sightings.

There are numerous tapes and CDs that can help you, and a portable CD player with headphones will allow you to compare quickly a live bird with an identified recording. The old-fashioned way to remember bird songs was to make up an English language version of the song. We've given you some of the classic renderings in the text that follows, such as *who...who cooks...you-all* as the call of the Barred Owl. Some of these phrases work better than others, however, especially since birds are prone to add or delete syllables from their calls, and very few birds pronounce consonants in a recognizable fashion. Making up your translations may work best of all.

Watching Bird Behavior: Some birders find that simply identifying and listing birds gives them satisfaction, but others would rather pursue particular species in detail and learn about their lives. The timing of migration is an easy thing to record, as are details of the feeding behavior, courtship and nesting of birds. Flocking birds can also provide fascinating opportunities to observe social interactions, especially when individual birds can be recognized.

One of the best ways to watch birds is to simply look for a bird-rich spot and sit quietly. The edges of forests or wetlands tend to be particularly productive. If you become part of the scenery, the birds will soon resume their activities.

23

Birding by Habitat: It is impossible to separate birds from their natural habitat—the combination of climate, landscape, plants and animals that provide a bird with its particular requirements for food and shelter. A bird's habitat is simply the sort of place in which it lives. Some prefer the open ocean, returning to land only to breed; others are found in cattail marshes; and still others in the tops of rainforest trees. By paying attention to the habitats of birds, you will not only find it easier to find particular species, but also much easier to identify birds, since they are rarely found outside their usual habitats. If you are birding in the mountains, you can afford to ignore the seabird section of this book. Out on a boat, don't worry much about the warblers.

Throughout this book, we have used a system of coded icons to illustrate the preferred habitats of each species of bird:

1) cities and suburbs and their typical landscapes, including gardens, parks and concrete jungles

2) open fields and farmland

3) water—meaning lakes and nearshore marine environments

4) marshes—typified by shallow water and plenty of emergent vegetation

5) rivers and streams

6) shorelines other than rocky ones

7) rocky shorelines

8) shrubby areas

9) the open ocean, far from land

10) lower elevation forests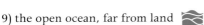

11) mountain forests

12) the alpine zone—above treeline in the mountains

13) the open sky

A quick glance at these icons will serve as a valuable double check to make sure your identifications are on the right track.

Calling Birds Closer: 'Pishing' and 'squeaking' are common strategies birdwatchers use to call birds in closer. Pishing simply involves making *psh-psh-psh* sounds with pursed lips, whereas squeaking is done by sucking on the back of your hand. There are also bird squeakers on the market that allow you to make attractive sounds without having to master these techniques. You could also try imitating the call of a Pygmy-Owl by whistling while trying to say *kook* about once every two to three seconds. These techniques work especially well for woodland songbirds such as chickadees and kinglets, although to the nonbirder they appear pretty bizarre. However, they are rapidly losing favor in the more crowded birding localities, since some people believe that the birds are spending more time investigating the birdwatchers than they are with the usual details of their own lives, which may lead to all manner of trouble for the birds.

Bird Listing: You can list as seriously or as casually as you like, or not at all, but lots of people enjoy keeping lists. When visiting a new area, a list becomes a souvenir of your experiences. Reviewing it, you can remember all sorts of details that made up the experience of your trip that day. Keeping regular accounts of birds in your home area can also become useful data for researchers, and it is interesting to compare the arrival dates and last sightings of hummingbirds and other seasonal visitors, or to note the first ever sighting of a new visitor to your area. There are computer bird list programs for those who are so inclined, but many naturalists simply keep records in field notebooks. Waterproof books and waterproof pens are a good idea for 'wet coast' birding, or you may find that a pocket dictaphone is all you need in the field, with a safe, dry notebook back home. Find a notebook that you like, and personalize it with field sketches, observations, poetry or what have you.

Birdwatching Groups and Activities: We also recommend that you join in on such activities as Christmas Bird Counts, birding festivals and the meetings of your local birding or natural history club. Meeting others with the same interests can make birding even more pleasurable, and there is always something to be learned in these sorts of situations.

Local bird hotlines may provide up-to-date information on sightings of rarities, which are often easier to relocate than you might think.

If you are interested in bird conservation and environmental issues—which usually involves trying to conserve their habitat—local groups can also put you in touch with the situation in your area and what you can do to help.

BIRD CONSERVATION

The West Coast is a good place to watch birds, especially when compared to the rest of the world. After all, there are still huge areas of more or less natural landscape here. Forestry, housing and agriculture development are threatening to make things progressively worse rather than better, but hopefully the more people there are that take up nature appreciation in the form of birding, the more friends the environment will have.

Birdwatchers have sometimes been accused of flagrantly spending money in the pursuit of seeing birds but not getting actively involved in conservation. We hope this tendency is changing. Many bird enthusiasts support groups such as Audubon, Ducks Unlimited, the Nature Trust and the Nature Conservancy, which assist bird conservation through such activities as buying and managing tracts of good habitat. In British Columbia, some communities have 'Big Day Birding Competitions,' which combine birding and conservation. Participants seek sponsors for every bird they see, and the proceeds go to the Nature Trust for the purchase of habitat.

On a local scale, consider landscaping your own property with attention to providing cover and natural foods for birds. The cumulative affects of such 'nature-scaping' can be significant. Remember, too, that millions of birds are killed by free-roaming house cats. House cats are called house cats for a reason.

Bird Feeding

Many people set up a backyard bird feeder in order to attract the birds to their yard. This activity is especially popular in winter, and it is possible to attract specific birds to your feeder by choosing the appropriate sort of seed or other food. The details of this process are discussed under the species that regularly visit feeders.

Consider keeping your feeder stocked through late spring. The weather may appear balmy, but before flowers bloom, seeds develop and insects hatch, birds may find springtime especially lean. When migratory birds return in early spring, resident birds must compete with them, and after a long winter, the pickings are especially slim. Extra food supplies at this time of year can be especially helpful.

Birdbaths are also a good way to bring birds to your yard, and it is increasingly popular to provide heated birdbaths during subzero weather in winter (a good idea, but you should avoid any designs with exposed metal parts, to which wet birds can accidentally freeze).

In summer the favorites of the bird-feeding crowd, the hummingbirds, can also be attracted to an appropriate location with a feeder offering artificial nectar. This nectar is a simple boiled sugar solution of three to four parts water to sugar.

In general, feeding birds is a good thing. There are many good books out on feeding birds and also about landscaping or nature-scaping your yard to provide natural foods and nest sites. We've listed a few of them at the back of the book.

Nest Boxes

The other popular method of attracting birds is to set out nest boxes, especially for wrens, chickadees, bluebirds and swallows. Not all birds will use nest boxes, since only species that naturally use tree hole cavities are comfortable in such confined spaces. It is a sad, but true, fact that the two most common bird species at both feeders and boxes are both non-native—the House Sparrow and the European Starling. For many people, the destruction of these birds (which admittedly do compete with native species) becomes a ruthless personal vendetta, although it is puzzling how anyone with an interest in birds can appreciate and enjoy some species while remorselessly killing others, especially when the 'others' are here to stay beyond any possible doubt.

Hummingbird Helpers

Watching hummingbirds at a feeder is enormously interesting. However, it's important to follow a few rules of hummingbird care.

• Boil up a sugar/water solution of 1:4 or 1:2.5 at the very richest. (Beyond that ratio the solution gets too viscous. Wild flower nectar is typically 1:4.)

• Red food coloring is unnecessary. Flag the area with red to first attract the birds—once they've found it, they'll remember.

• Don't use honey—it can cause fungal growths in the hummingbird.

• Change the solution every few days in the heat of summer—it ferments. Wash the feeder with boiling water every time you add new solution.

• Once you start, keep it up, since the birds may be depending on you. The specialized food requirements of hummingbirds make them more prone to becoming dependent on feeders than most seed-eating birds.

• Visit wild bird nature stores for lots of good advice, or pick up *Attracting Backyard Wildlife* by Bill Merilees. He goes beyond feeders and tells you how to plant nectar-producing plants that bloom in succession.

Winter Weather Bird Feeding Tips

• Avoid letting the seeds get wet. Moisture makes seeds impossible for the birds to husk. If possible, put out only a day or two's supply at a time.

• Look for dry spots to sprinkle seeds, or lay down a board on the snow. Supplement millet and sunflower seed with raisins and apples.

• Hang a suet feeder or fill pinecones with peanut butter. Suet is like a power bar for birds.

• Birds need water for drinking—they can metabolize snow, but it's a waste of calories. Put out a pan of hot water or buy a thermostatically controlled heater. Don't add anything to the water because if birds splash in it, their feathers may lose their insulating properties.

• Please delay spraying trees and gardens with dormant oil spray, a lime-sulfur mixture that kills wintering insect eggs and larvae. Delaying forever would be good—birds are natural insecti-cides—but at least wait until the hardest part of winter is over.

• Once you start feeding birds, keep it up through late spring because the pressure on resident birds to find food increases when the migratory birds return.

The BIRDS

COMMON LOON  cW - Pendov
Gavia immer

YELLOW-BILLED LOON
Gavia adamsii

Common Loons are dagger-billed, goose-sized divers that swim low in the water and have a smooth, noncrested head. Their plumage is black and white in summer; brown and white in winter. Rare Yellow-billed Loons have a paler bill and neck in winter plumage. Pacific and Red-throated Loons are smaller and slimmer.

Common Loon: **breeding**

Although Common Loons are the most abundant loon in the Pacific Northwest, they are common in name alone. In summer they live on large, deep lakes that have plenty of fish and other aquatic creatures to eat. There they give voice to their classic wailing cries. They nest on quiet shorelines, and their one or two eggs hatch into precocious, little chicks that like to ride on their parents' backs. Loons' waterfront nests are easily damaged by boat wakes. It is rare to find loons breeding in Washington and Oregon anymore, although they are still reasonably successful in B.C.

By late summer Common Loons assemble into flocks, and the fall migration, which brings thousands of birds to protected coastal waters, is more or less over by the end of September. The Fraser River estuary and the Strait of Juan de Fuca are popular destinations for winter loons once ice cover locks them out of their summer homes. This is the time to begin scanning for Yellow-bellied Loons that have strayed here from Alaska.

Common Loon: *non-breeding*

Seasonal Occurrence & Local Range: *Common Loons are found throughout the Pacific Northwest, on freshwater lakes in summer and protected salt water in winter. Yellow-billed Loons breed on tundra lakes and are seen on the West Coast as rare winter vagrants. 'Looning' peaks during the April to May migration and in winter, when these birds concentrate in coastal waters.*
Size: *both about 80 cm (32 in).*

PACIFIC LOON
Gavia pacifica

Pender - cw

The Pacific Loon is smaller and finer billed than the Common Loon. The winter adult is white below and dark brown above, with a horizontal bill. In winter this loon shows a straight border between the dark back and light front of the neck, whereas the Common Loon's border is messy. In summer the Pacific Loon has a velvety gray head, a dark throat and a checkered back.

Pacific Loon: *non-breeding*

Pacific Loons arrive in fall from their northern breeding grounds, still sporting their lustrous, gray head and an iridescent throat patch. In the right light this patch is scintillating purple in color, but sadly, from most angles, it appears dull black. By November these birds wear the drab brown and white garb of winter and tend to hang out in flocks, unlike antisocial Common and Red-throated Loons. Preferring tide rips and areas of powerful currents, they dive in search of fish, surfacing to swallow them triumphantly. In April and May you can sometimes see hundreds of these gorgeous, gray-headed divers in the seething waters of Active Pass on the ferry run between Victoria and Vancouver. They are also seen in great numbers around the Queen Charlotte Islands in May.

North America's largest wintering population is in the San Juans and Gulf Islands. Pacific Loons were previously called Arctic Loons, but it is now understood, thanks to the diligence of our ornithological comrades in Siberia, that they are two separate but almost identical species.

Seasonal Occurrence & Local Range: *Pacific Loons winter in coastal waters from Alaska to Baja, from September through June.*
Size: *about 66 cm (26 in.).*

RED-THROATED LOON
Gavia stellata

The 'Red-throat' is a small, very slender loon that holds its bill uptilted. In summer it has a gray back, red throat and striped nape. In winter its pale gray plumage is less distinctive than its uptilted bill.

Red-throated Loon: *non-breeding*

Red-throated Loons are the slimmest of our loons. Along the coast we usually see them only in winter plumage, fishing close to shore in estuaries and bays. Because of their washed-out, motley colors, they are easily overlooked. In winter they are fairly common near Puget Sound and in the Strait of Georgia. The Fraser River delta is an especially good spot to search for all of our loon species and to practice sorting them out before they head north to breed in the spring.

Loons fly hunchbacked with their necks dangling, legs trailing behind and wings beating rapidly; yet despite all awkward appearances, they cover long distances on migration. Loons are heavy birds with solid, rather than hollow, bones that are great for diving but not much help in the air. Red-throats are the only loons that are able to take off without a long, skittering taxi. This ability enables them to nest on small ponds in their northern breeding grounds and fly off to feed on larger lakes or even to the ocean.

Seasonal Occurrence & Local Range: *Red-throated Loons winter along the coast from the Aleutians to Baja and can be seen September through May.* **Size:** *about 64 cm (25 in.).*

 WESTERN GREBE
Aechmophorus occidentalis

CLARK'S GREBE
Aechmophorus clarkii

Grebes are smaller and longer necked than loons. They have slim, pointed bills and a somewhat cobra-shaped head. The Western Grebe is a long-billed, swan-necked water bird; the black above is crisply separated from the white below.

Western Grebe: *adult*

With their long, snake-like necks, ruby eyes and a stiletto bill for piercing fish, Western Grebes are very scary-looking birds. When sexes look alike, as in this species, mate selection is often made on the basis of behavior, and Western Grebes are famous for their courtship dances, during which they skitter spectacularly across the water's surface. Seeing this display is well worth an inland field trip since these birds almost never breed on the coast.

Western Grebes are extremely susceptible to human disturbance, and only a few breeding colonies remain on inland lakes in B.C. and Washington. Migrating Western Grebes have also been known to land on wet pavement, mistaking it for water. Since they can't walk—their legs are too far back—or take off from land, this error can have serious consequences. More Western Grebes winter near Vancouver than anywhere else in the world, with up to 15,000 birds in huge rafts on English Bay.

Clark's Grebe was formerly considered one species with the Western Grebe, but this rare visitor can be distinguished by a black cap that doesn't quite cover the eye and a pale orange rather than yellow bill.

Seasonal Occurrence & Local Range: *Both species winter along the coast, especially in Georgia Strait and Puget Sound. They arrive in mid-September and leave by mid-May.*
Size: *both about 64 cm (25 in.).*

33

PIED-BILLED GREBE
Podilymbus podiceps

A small grebe, the Pied-billed is a short-necked, big-headed, thick-billed, brown diving bird of inland lakes. It is really quite difficult to mistake for any other grebe, or any other freshwater bird for that matter, except perhaps the American Coot.

Pied-billed Grebe: *breeding*

Pied-billed grebes are the oddballs of the grebe family. Their sturdy, white bill has a thick black ring in summer—hence the name 'pied-billed.' Typically loners, they are squat, little submarines that can sink with nary a ripple, just by compressing their feathers. Once you spot them, they keep you busy lifting and lowering your binoculars as they disappear in a blink, popping up unexpectedly elsewhere, or vanishing completely into the reeds.

Pied-billed Grebes are homebodies that like to lurk year-round on the same pond or marsh, weather permitting. Often the first clue to their presence is a loud, whooping *kuk-kuk-cow-cow-cow-cowp-cowp*. If you see them on salt water, it's likely the result of a cold snap that has forced them away from their preferred inland haunts.

Pied-billed Grebes are not strictly fish eaters, and they can survive on a variety of aquatic critters. When incubating, they often leave their eggs covered with decomposing nesting material, which keeps the eggs warm in their absence.

Seasonal Occurrence & Local Range: *The Pied-billed Grebe breeds locally from central B.C. southward and winters from southern B.C. through the coastal states. It is found year-round on open water; there is some fall migration from inland waters to the coast.*
Size: *about 33 cm (13 in.).*

RED-NECKED GREBE
Podiceps grisegena

The Red-necked Grebe is a medium-sized, long-billed, long-necked, cobra-headed water bird. In the summer it has silver cheeks and a red neck. In the winter it is a grubby gray-brown bird, not neatly black and white like the Western Grebe.

Red-necked Grebe: *breeding*

As you wander by the seashore in winter, listen for a rasping *kraaaagh*, and watch for the Red-necked Grebe—with no sign of a red neck. In summer this bird is a real looker with its flared head, neat white chin and vermilion-colored neck, but in winter it wears the dull grays and browns of coastal days.

Occasionally, during migration, large groups of Red-necked Grebes search for fish in places like Puget Sound and around Vancouver Island, but they don't usually fraternize with other grebe species. More often, one Red-necked Grebe fishes near a group of scoters or other sea ducks. The Red-necked Grebe is about the size of the ducks it hangs out with, but the Horned Grebe, with which it could be confused, is much tinier.

Red-necked Grebes breed on inland waters. Although their eggs are a lovely light blue when first laid, nest materials soon stain them blotchy brown, camouflaging them from predators.

Seasonal Occurrence & Local Range: *This grebe winters along the coast from Alaska as far south as California. It is common along the coast from October though April.*
Size: *about 46 cm (18 in.).*

HORNED GREBE
Podiceps auritus

EARED GREBE
Podiceps nigricollis

The Horned Grebe is a small grebe with a small, sharp bill and a white cheek and throat contrasting with a black cap and back. On expansive ocean waters in winter, it appears strikingly small in comparison to the other birds that share this habitat. The uncommon Eared Grebe is best recognized by its darker cheek and dusky throat.

Horned Grebe: *non-breeding*

Like many seabirds that winter on the coast, Horned Grebes lose the splendor of their summer plumage and assume low-key black and whites. Only one touch of color remains, in their blazing, ruby red eyes.

Horned Grebes are the most abundant winter grebe in the San Juans and are common in shallow, protected bays along the B.C. coast from September through March. They can be distinguished by their small size and peppy behavior as they pop into the air to dive and disappear neatly headfirst. If you are lucky, you may occasionally see a group of four or five grebes dive together as a team, herding fishes.

Eared Grebes are close in size to Horned Grebes but are much less common. Both nest on inland freshwater lakes and ponds, on floating platforms of plant material, in typical grebe fashion.

Seasonal Occurrence & Local Range: *Both species are widespread winter visitors to our area, although the Horned Grebe is much more abundant than the Eared Grebe.*
Size: *Horned: about 34 cm (13.5 in.); Eared: about 32 cm (12.5 in.).*

BROWN PELICAN
Pelecanus occidentalis

A huge, dark bird soaring over the sea with a long, pouched bill and its head crooked back over its shoulders is almost certainly a Brown Pelican.

Brown Pelican: *breeding*

Brown Pelicans are not common along the Northwest Coast, and in B.C. they are downright rare. However, in a few localities, such as Westport, Washington, you can see hundreds of these magnificent birds each fall. They are not local breeders, but they are powerful fliers and wander great distances in search of food, especially after the breeding season is over.

Pelicans are related to cormorants, and like them they have webbing joining all four toes, and a throat pouch. Of course, the pelican's throat pouch dwarfs that of the cormorant, and if you are lucky enough to see a pelican dive nearby into clear water, you will be amazed when the bird's bill suddenly swells to the size of a beachball. After the dive the water is expelled, and the fish within are swallowed. Pelicans are also remarkably graceful fliers, with the ability to soar high on thermal currents or glide effortlessly just a few finger widths over the water surface.

North America's only other pelican, the American White Pelican, is found along the Northwest Coast only rarely. It is white with black wing tips, and it almost never dives for fish.

Seasonal Occurrence & Range: *The Brown Pelican is an uncommon wanderer from southern B.C. southwards; it is seen mainly in the fall.*
Size: *about 125 cm (50 in.).*

CORMORANTS

PELAGIC CORMORANT
Phalacrocorax pelagicus

DOUBLE-CRESTED CORMORANT
Phalacrocorax auritus

BRANDT'S CORMORANT
Phalacrocorax penicillatus

Cormorants are dark, goose-sized, long-necked, long-billed seabirds. They often stand upright and hold their wings out to dry. Pelagics are generally slimmer and smaller than the other two species and have two big white patches on their flanks in breeding season. Double-crested Cormorants are stockier, fly with a kink in the neck and have a yellow throat year-round. Brandt's have a blue throat in spring, a pale chin strap line and an unkinked neck in flight.

Pelagic Cormorant: *breeding*

Cormorants typically are seen flying in single file, floating low in the water, or hanging out on rocks or pilings with wings outspread to dry. It seems bizarre for a seabird to lack waterproofing, but the cormorant's ability to wet its feathers also decreases its buoyancy, making it easier for the bird to dive deeply and chase the fish on which it feeds.

Double-crested Cormorant: *breeding*

All cormorants are colonial nesters. Pelagics breed on rocky cliff faces, inaccessible to most predators. You can walk right underneath an active colony along the Stanley Park seawall in Vancouver. If you can stand the smell, you can pause to be entertained by the cormorants landing and leaping from their impossibly tiny ledge nest sites, which are little more than bits of seaweed glued together by guano.

If you see a cormorant inland or on fresh water, it is almost surely a Double-crested. Populations of this cormorant have been on the rise in B.C. and Washington, and three-quarters of the B.C. population nests on Mandarte and Chain islands near Victoria.

Strictly coastal, Brandt's Cormorants seek out tidal rips and areas of current such as Active Pass in the Gulf Islands and Cattle Island in the San Juans. The number of breeding Brandt's Cormorants seems to fluctuate greatly from year to year in the Pacific Northwest.

Brandt's Cormorant: *breeding*

Seasonal Occurrence & Local Range: *Pelagics and Double-cresteds are found all along the coast. Brandt's typically migrate north after breeding, and thousands come north from California in the fall to winter in B.C. and Washington.*
Size: *Pelagic: about 69 cm (27 in.); Double-crested and Brandt's: about 86 cm (34 in.).*

BLACK-FOOTED ALBATROSS

Diomedea nigripes

Black-footed Albatrosses are sooty-colored seabirds whose long, thin wings span almost two meters (seven feet). They fly stiffly, frequently banking from side to side. The young birds are darkest; older birds become paler on the head and neck.

Black-footed Albatross: *adult*

Albatrosses, shearwaters, petrels and fulmars share a seafaring lifestyle. We tend to think of these pelagic birds as rare, but that's because we seldom visit their habitat. Only at close range is it possible to spot the tubular nostrils protruding above the bill, the feature that accounts for them collectively being called 'tubenoses.' Their tubenoses are associated with salt glands that enable them to drink salt water.

You almost have to be an Ancient Mariner to see albatrosses because they seldom venture near shore, although they are attracted to boats and will follow them hoping for handouts. These impressive birds feed by picking translucent squid and shimmering fish off the surface. They have frequently been victims of floating garbage, particularly plastics, which to them must resemble their food.

Seasonal Occurrence & Local Range: *Black-footed Albatrosses are most commonly seen in summer and fall. They sometimes concentrate offshore of Washington in the fall, possibly to prepare for their return to their breeding grounds in the Hawaiian Islands. They can be seen offshore of the Queen Charlotte Islands, particularly in stormy weather, gliding effortlessly on their narrow, pointed wings.*
Size: *91 cm (36 in.), with a 200-cm (80-in.) wingspan.*

 **NORTHERN FULMAR**
Fulmarus glacialis

Fulmars look superficially like the archetypal gull, but their flight pattern is a distinctive, stiff-winged flapping punctuated with soaring glides, in contrast to the looser flapping of gulls. They are also more thick necked than gulls and hold their thick, yellowish bill angled downward. They come in different color forms ranging from dark gray to almost white, and in the North Pacific more than half are dark phase birds.

Northern Fulmar: *adult*

Northern Fulmar are abundant birds in the offshore waters of British Columbia and Washington. They are attracted to the offal of fishing boats but can easily be overlooked in a crowd of gulls and shearwaters. Look for their arthritic wing flapping, which is one of the best ways to pick them out.

Fulmars nest in colonies on island cliffs in the far north. When disturbed, they have the discomfiting habit of retching fish oil. The vile stuff is an effective deterrent to most predators and is actually a common feature of the tube-nosed swimmers in general. This 'eau de Fulmar' has more staying power than the most expensive man-made perfumes. If sprayed on other birds, this revolting stuff can destroy their waterproofing and lead to waterlogging, hypothermia and even drowning.

Seasonal Occurrence & Local Range: *Northern Fulmars are most abundant offshore from fall through early spring as they head north to Alaska to breed.*
Size: *about 46 cm (18 in.), with a 107-cm (42-in.) wingspan.*

41

SHEARWATERS

SOOTY SHEARWATER
Puffinus griseus

PINK-FOOTED SHEARWATER
Puffinus creatopus

Shearwaters resemble gulls with long, thin, stiffly held wings. They fly in a roller coaster flight pattern and are often seen in huge numbers. Sooty Shearwaters are quite gray overall; Pink-footed Shearwaters are light on the underside, and their legs and bill are pink, not gray.

Sooty Shearwater: *adult*

The sight of thousands of shearwaters, swirling and feeding in a flowing river of life across the seas, is not soon forgotten. But unless you are well out to sea, you are unlikely to see them. As wide ranging as the oceans themselves, Sooty Shearwaters breed on islands off New Zealand, Australia and South America. In spring they pour north towards their winter feeding grounds in Alaska.

Shearwaters fly with several flaps upward, then soar down the troughs between waves, plucking food off the surface or plunging into the water to seize fish and shrimp below the surface. They rely on wind and their great gliding ability to travel vast distances. If becalmed, they simply float on the water until the winds make travel possible once more.

Pink-footed Shearwaters are less commonly seen than 'Sooties' off the West Coast, and as you go farther out to sea, you increase your chances of seeing rare Flesh-footed, Buller's and Short-tailed Shearwaters as well.

Seasonal Occurrence & Local Range: *The subadult Sooty Shearwaters move through en route to Alaska in March and April, followed by the adults in May. They begin their southern migration to their breeding grounds in late August. Pink-footed Shearwaters stay well offshore and may be seen from July through September as they make their back to their Chilean breeding grounds.*
Size: *both about 48 cm (19 in.), with a 109-cm (43-in.) wingspan.*

STORM-PETRELS

FORK-TAILED STORM-PETREL
Oceanodroma furcata

LEACH'S STORM-PETREL
Oceanodroma leucorhoa

Storm-Petrels are small, pelagic birds that fly with shallow wing beats interspersed with glides. Forked-tailed Storm-Petrels are bluish gray above and pearly gray below. Leach's Storm-Petrels are darker, with a slightly notched tail, a divided, white rump patch and more erratic flight.

Fork-tailed Storm-Petrel: *adult*

These birds are sometimes called 'sea swallows' because of their diminutive size and fluttering flight. Storm-Petrels were so named by mariners who believed that their presence near their ships foretold an approaching storm. 'Petrel' comes from St. Peter who, so the story goes, once tried to walk on water: Storm-Petrels dangle their feet and patter over the water, all the while snatching up bits of floating food.

Fork-tailed Storm-Petrels can follow the scent of fish oil on the water to its source, usually a fishing boat or fish factory. In the days when canneries dotted the coastline, these birds could be seen over inshore waters, but they normally prefer to stay offshore. However, in September there is a regular migration of 'Fork-tails' through Johnstone and Georgia straits.

Leach's Storm-Petrels equal Fork-tails in number, but they forage mainly at night far offshore. They nest in mixed colonies with Fork-tails.

Seasonal Occurrence & Local Range: *Fork-tailed Storm-Petrels breed along the outer coast and in the Queen Charlottes. Washington is at the southern end of their breeding range. They are seen most often March through November. The nocturnal Leach's are seldom seen.*
Size: *both about 20 cm (8 in.).*

COMMON MURRE
Uria aalge

The auk family, or 'alcids,' are in some ways the northern versions of penguins. They are stocky, small, black and white diving birds with small wings designed for underwater flying in pursuit of fish. Common Murres are the sleekest, most sharp billed of the large alcids. In winter they have white cheeks and a dark line through the eye.

Common Murre: *breeding*

Like other alcids, Common Murres are true seabirds that only come ashore to breed. They fly with rapid wing beats and swerve, their large feet acting as rudders.

In summer Common Murres are locally concentrated in huge colonies on cliff faces. They forego the usual niceties of a nest, and instead, they rest their single egg on large, webbed feet to incubate it, relying on the shape of the egg to prevent it from rolling off the cliff. When nudged, the pointy egg pivots in a tight circle.

The black upper surface and white underside of murres and other alcids is called counter shading and is believed to camouflage them from their prey and predators, including killer whales and sea lions. The birds' bellies blend in against the lightness of the sky, and their backs match the dark sea depths.

Murre colonies are found along the outer coast, but a number of these birds appear in Puget Sound and the Strait of Georgia in late summer and fall as they disperse from the colonies.

Seasonal Occurrence & Local Range: *Common Murres are found all along the coast. Widespread and abundant in winter, these birds move to inaccessible cliffside breeding colonies in summer.*
Size: *about 43 cm (17 in.).*

PIGEON GUILLEMOT
Cepphus columba

Somewhat similar in shape to a Common Murre, Pigeon Guillemots are smaller and solid black, with a big white wing patch. Their bright red feet are unmistakable. In winter the head turns white with a dark eye stripe, the black body turns a mottled gray, and the white wing patch remains.

Pigeon Guillemot: *breeding*

Pigeon Guillemots are the alcid most commonly seen close to shore and in protected waters. They nest in crevices in rocks and often can be seen standing around in twosomes or small groups. In their summer courtship rituals, they flirt outrageously, waving their scarlet feet, whistling wheezily and peering down each others' throats—which are as red as their feet.

Like all alcids, Pigeon Guillemots are better designed for flying underwater than in air. Their small wings are used for propulsion while swimming (they pursue fish underwater, as do other alcids) and push them along speedily. But in the air, guillemots must patter across the surface of the water a long time before they can lift their red landing gear and become airborne.

Despite their name, these birds are not particularly pigeon-like, and the word 'guillemot' is apparently derived from an informal French version of the name William.

Seasonal Occurrence & Local Range: *Pigeon Guillemots are found all along the coast, year-round.*
Size: *about 33 cm (13 in.).*

FANCY-BEAKED ALCIDS

TUFTED PUFFIN
Fratercula cirrhata

HORNED PUFFIN
Fratercula corniculata

RHINOCEROS AUKLET
Cerorhinca monocerata

Puffins are black with a white face and an eye-popping, thick, orange bill. Tufted Puffins are black bellied and have blonde face tufts; the rare Horned Puffins have a white belly and no tufts. Rhinoceros Auklets are stubby, dark brown birds with two white face stripes and a pale bill spike in the breeding season.

Tufted Puffin: *breeding*

With their comical beaks and cavalier head tufts, Tufted Puffins are one of the most popular birds of the West Coast. You really have to go looking for them though, since they have very specific breeding site requirements. They nest on remote rocky islands with grassy areas into which they can burrow. They are most often seen flying furiously to and from their nesting sites, their huge bills cutting an unmistakable silhouette. Cape Flattery, Lopez Island in the San Juans, whale-watching tours in Clayoquot Sound, Cannon Beach in Oregon and the south end of the Queen Charlotte Islands are all good bets for puffin watching.

Horned Puffins can be found in only a few out-of-the-way places, such as the Queen Charlotte Islands. They resemble the Atlantic Puffin of the east coast—a familiar bird that is often the subject of nature art and photography.

In recent years puffins have had a tough time of it—they are extremely dependent on small fish of a very specific size, and the U.S. Fish and Wildlife Service has estimated that 27 percent of the puffins living off the Pacific coast are drowned annually in fishermen's gill nets.

Rhinoceros Auklets also grow fancy bits on their faces in breeding season: their wispy, white face plumes become more pronounced and they grow a thick, rhino-style spike on top of the base of the bill, which falls off later in the season.

Rhinoceros Auklet: *breeding*

Seasonal Occurrence & Local Range: *Puffins are locally abundant in summer, but spend the winter hundreds of kilometers offshore. Rhinoceros Auklets are commonly seen in summer all along the coast. In winter they are rare in northern B.C. but remain rather common in Puget Sound.* **Size:** *all about 38 cm (15 in.).*

SMALL ALCIDS

MARBLED MURRELET
Brachyramphus marmoratus

ANCIENT MURRELET
Synthliboramphus antiquus

CASSIN'S AUKLET 〰
Ptychoramphus aleuticus

The Marbled Murrelets' tiny size, stubby tail and brown-barred summer plumage are distinctive. Unlike grebes, they don't leap when they dive, and they appear neckless. In winter they turn black and white. Ancient Murrelets are larger but otherwise similar in winter, although they lack a white stripe along the wing. In breeding plumage they show a white line across the temples. Cassin's Auklets appear small and uniformly dusky, their white belly seen only in flight.

Marbled Murrelet: *breeding*

For years the nesting site of the little Marbled Murrelets was a mystery, though perhaps their cryptic, grouse-like coloring should have given us a clue. It turns out that Marbled Murrelets hide their nests in mossy clumps high in giant, old growth trees. After nesting season, they change their forest camouflage to the typical black and white, counter-shaded camouflage of other alcids. Marbled Murrelets can be seen feeding fairly close to

Ancient Murrelet: *breeding*

shore, almost always in multiples of two. Sea kayakers commonly enjoy the sight of these perky, little seabirds popping up beside their boats and then diving bottoms up in great haste.

Ancient Murrelets are so called because of the floppy, white feathers that extend above the eye like an old man's bushy white eyebrows. In the Queen Charlotte Islands, Ancient Murrelets have maintained a major nesting area in burrows at the base of old growth trees. The adults exchange incubation duty under the cover of darkness, and the precocious chicks dash to the sea only two days after hatching, without ever having been fed on land.

Like the Ancient Murrelets, the small, mostly dark Cassin's Auklets breed on offshore islands where they are only active at night. If seen on the water, their distinctive markings are a white spot above the eye and a pale spot on the lower mandible. Their plumage is the same year-round.

Cassin's Auklet: *adult*

Seasonal Occurrence & Local Range: *These three species can be found all along the outer coast, but not in the Strait of Georgia and Puget Sound. They are very commonly seen April through August near shore, but disperse more widely at sea in winter.*
Size: *all about 24 cm (9.5 in.).*

JAEGERS

PARASITIC JAEGER
Stercorarius parasiticus

LONG-TAILED JAEGER
Stercorarius longicaudus

POMARINE JAEGER
Stercorarius pomarinus

Jaegers are dark, gull-like birds with long, pointed, falcon-like wings. On Parasitic Jaegers, the most common species, the two elongated central tail feathers are pointed and stick out a few finger widths beyond the tail. The Long-tailed Jaeger has two long streamers instead, and the Pomarine has broad, rounded tips to these feathers. Immature jaegers are much more difficult to identify.

Parasitic Jaeger: *light phase, adult*

'Jaeger' means 'hunter' in German, but along the West Coast, jaegers are best known as pirates. They are fancy-flying members of the gull and tern group that have taken to stealing food from other gull family members.

Jaegers terrorize gulls and terns, twisting and turning in spectacular high-speed chases, until the exhausted birds either drop or vomit their hard-earned food. On their tundra breeding grounds, jaegers typically hunt lemmings, but they have been known to trail ornithologists in bird colonies, picking eggs out of nests where the brooding parents have been disturbed. Given the opportunity, jaegers will feed themselves until they are so heavy they have to disgorge their food to fly.

In autumn jaegers can sometimes be seen from shore, trailing flocks of migrating gulls, in search of easy pickings. Watch for a dark bird cleaving aggressively through a flock of paler gulls, and be sure to check to see if it is a rare Long-tailed or Pomarine Jaeger.

Seasonal Occurrence & Local Range: *Jaegers migrate along the coast in spring and fall, but they are more often spotted during their fall migration. Parasitic Jaegers are most common close to shore, whereas Long-tailed and Pomarine Jaegers migrate far offshore.*
Size: *Parasitic Jaeger: about 48 cm (19 in.); Long-tailed: about 56 cm (22 in.); Pomarine: about 53 cm (21 in.).*

HEERMANN'S GULL
Larus heermanni

Heermann's Gulls have a subtle beauty. No other species is smoky gray with a contrasting blood red bill. In flight they are swift, light and agile. In contrast, the common bigger gulls, which are heavy and powerful, row rather than sail through the air.

Heermann's Gull: *non-breeding*

The Heermann's is one of the few true 'sea gulls,' found over salt water whenever it isn't on land to breed. This is not a gull that you will find at city parks and garbage dumps. For us, this species is a fall bird, and it is most often seen along the outer coast. Oddly enough, its breeding grounds are south of here (near Baja California) rather than north. The birds disperse both north and south after nesting is over.

Heermann's are 'three year gulls,' meaning it takes them three years to acquire their exquisite adult plumage. Ring-billed and Mew Gulls also take three years, but the big gulls require four. Young Heermann's share the adults' mastery of flight and are usually identifiable by their dark sooty color, but to fully appreciate this species one needs to see a grown-up bird. Unfortunately, the breeding plumage, in which the head is white rather than speckled, is rarely encountered this far north.

Renowned as robbers, these birds steal food from pelicans and members of the booby family, but this far north these targets are rare, and the gulls get most of their food from the water's surface.

Seasonal Occurrence & Local Range: *Heermann's Gulls are seen along the outer coast from August through November.*
Size: *about 48 cm (19 in.).*

PINK-LEGGED GULLS

GLAUCOUS-WINGED GULL
Larus glaucescens

WESTERN GULL
Larus occidentalis

GLAUCOUS GULL
Larus hyperboreus

The big-billed Glaucous-winged Gull, with gray wing tips, is the common gull of the British Columbia coast, and the dark-backed Western Gull takes its place from Oregon south. The much more rare Glaucous Gull is lighter-colored all around, with white wing tips.

Glaucous-winged Gull: *breeding*

Gulls are great birds to watch—graceful in flight, voracious when feeding and capable of a huge variety of sounds and body language when negotiating with one another. They are most amusing in their huge breeding colonies—a spectacle many birders never see.

Gulls can also be some of the toughest birds to identify, and it often comes as a shock to beginners that there is no such species as the 'sea gull' and that a dozen similar species have equal claim to that name. With the Glaucous-winged and Western Gulls, identification is complicated by the fact that the two species interbreed, producing birds with the characteristics of both species and coincidentally resembling Thayer's Gulls as well. The light-colored Glaucous-winged Gulls are easy to recognize (and they are much less light than the rare Glaucous Gulls), as are the dark Westerns. Honest birders will admit defeat with many of the intermediates, however. Brownish or gray-speckled youngsters are yet another story, so here we will concentrate only on the neatly patterned adults.

Western Gull: *breeding*

Seasonal Occurrence & Local Range: *Glaucous-winged Gulls are found year-round on the B.C. and north Washington coasts, some dispersing south in winter. Western Gulls breed from central Washington south, and some disperse north in winter to B.C. Glaucous Gulls are generally winter visitors.* **Size:** *all about 66 cm (26 in.).*

MORE PINK-LEGGED GULLS

HERRING GULL
Larus argentatus

THAYER'S GULL
Larus thayeri

GLAUCOUS-WINGED–
WESTERN GULL HYBRID
Larus glaucescens x occidentalis

Herring Gulls are almost as large as the gulls on pages 52 and 53, with a lighter back than Western Gulls and darker wing tips than Glaucous-winged Gulls (like a larger, pink-legged version of the yellowish-legged gulls). Thayer's resemble Herring Gulls but have a dark, rather than yellow, eye and a finer bill. Glaucous-winged–Western Gull hybrids are gray-backed with dark wing tips and dark eyes—much like Thayer's Gulls but with a heavier bill.

Herring Gull: *non-breeding*

OK, so what's going on here—why so many species of nearly identical gulls? Well, what we are seeing is the result of a relatively recent evolutionary divergence from what was probably a widespread ancestral gull that is now distinctive in many parts of its range—distinctive enough to be divided into separate species. The species that can trace their origins to this ancestor include the Herring, Thayer's, Glaucous-winged, Western, Glaucous, Yellow-legged and Iceland Gulls, and all of them can either interbreed or resemble one another from time to time.

The pink-legged gulls are large enough to be formidable predators on animals as large as young birds, and all of them seem to enjoy a trip to the local dump as well. For birders, this presents a great opportunity for study and challenge, since nowhere else are gulls this abundant and diverse. Still, you have to ask yourself just how much time you want to spend at the landfill sites gull watching, or whether the gulls you see on the shoreline will suffice to pique your interest in this complex group of birds.

Thayer's Gull: *non-breeding*

Seasonal Occurrence & Local Range: Herring and Thayer's Gulls are primarily winter visitors in this area. Glaucous-winged–Western Gull hybrids are also seen mainly in winter throughout the region but especially along the outer coasts of Washington and Oregon.
Size: *Herring and hybrids: about 66 cm (26 in.); Thayer's: about 58 cm (23 in.).*

YELLOWISH-LEGGED GULLS

CALIFORNIA GULL
Larus californicus

RING-BILLED GULL
Larus delawarensis

MEW GULL
Larus canus

These gulls all have gray backs, white undersides and black-tipped wings. California Gulls are the largest, with a longish bill marked with both a black and a red spot, and yellow-greenish legs. Ring-billed Gulls are rounder headed, with a black-ringed bill and yellow legs. The smallest of the three, Mew Gulls have a dainty head and a finer, all-yellow bill, which in younger birds is dark at the tip, often leading to confusion with 'Ring-bills.'

California Gull: *breeding*

Like most gulls, Californias will gobble down just about anything they can manage. In 1848, when Utah was besieged by a plague of crop-devouring crickets, huge flocks of California Gulls showed up and devoured the pests. To this day, the Mormons remain grateful, and so the California Gull is actually the state bird of Utah.

Wheeling and hovering flocks of Ring-bills are abundant in dumps over much of their range and are commonly seen in parks and farmlands, and along lakeshores, most abundantly during spring and fall migration, although they can be seen in any month.

Mew Gulls, named for their calls, behave more like shorebirds than other gulls, eschewing dumps in favor of plowed fields and mud flats, where they probe for food with their beaks. In general, the smaller the gull, the more refined its behavior.

Juvenile gulls are always confusing, leaving beginning birders to reflect on why these youngsters not only change feathers with maturation but often bill and leg color too. Still, long after a birdwatcher memorizes other species, he or she can still find challenging gulls to identify, since often no two individuals seem to look the same.

Ring-billed Gull: *non-breeding*

Mew Gull: *breeding*

Seasonal Occurrence & Local Range: California Gulls migrate to the coast from late June to November and head back inland in March and April. Ring-billed Gulls are most common in summer. Mew Gulls are uncommon breeders on forested lakes along the B.C. coast and common winter visitors.
Size: *California: about 51 cm (20 in.); Ring-billed Gull: about 48 cm (19 in.); Mew Gull: about 46 cm (18 in.).*

SMALL GULLS

BONAPARTE'S GULL
Xema sabini

SABINE'S GULL
Larus philadelphia

BLACK-LEGGED KITTIWAKE
Rissa tridactyla

These small gulls are delicate in both form and habits, and none is likely to be found at the dump. In winter, when they are most often seen, Bonaparte's Gulls have a mostly white head and a white wedge on the leading edge of the wing, Sabine's Gulls have a gray head and a three-toned wing, and Black-legged Kittiwakes look like black-legged Mew Gulls with no white in the black wing tips. Bonaparte's are usually black faced in spring. In fall they sport only a black beauty spot on the cheek.

Bonaparte's Gull: *breeding*

Black-legged Kittiwakes are seabirds that only occasionally venture near river mouths and coastal shores, sometimes after storms or on migration. Likewise, Sabine's Gulls are much more common offshore than they are along the coast, and both species pass through our area mainly on migration. The adults are easy to distinguish, but young birds share a similar look in flight.

Bonaparte's Gulls are a much more common sight, and this species is an inland breeder that comes to the coast in winter and migrates through in large flocks spring and fall. It is the most abundant of the small, delicate gulls, and for those naturalists who feel some disdain for the gulls, time spent watching Bonaparte's Gulls is the surest way to be won over. The arrival of the scratchy-voiced Bonaparte's in March is an early sign of spring. By August they are trickling past again, most wintering south of the border.

Bonaparte's Gull: *non-breeding*

Seasonal Occurrence & Local Range*: All are winter visitors or migrants, although Sabine's are rarely seen in winter, and except for the Bonaparte's, are most likely to be seen offshore or along the outer coast.*
Size: *Bonaparte's and Sabine's: about 33 cm (13 in.); Kittiwake: about 43 cm (17 in.)*

TERNS

CASPIAN TERN
Sterna caspia

COMMON TERN
Sterna hirundo

ARCTIC TERN
Sterna paradisaea

Terns resemble gulls, but they are slimmer, fork tailed and sharp billed. Caspian Terns are huge with a heavy, red bill tipped with black. Common Terns' bills are also tipped with black, but the bird is more petite overall. In flight Common Terns show a gray wedge on the tips of the upper wings, but the Arctic Terns' wings are uniformly gray and their bill is solid red.

Caspian Tern: *breeding*

Terns fly buoyantly on pointed wings, their heads tilted downwards as they scan the water for fish. Then, plummeting downward, they dive headfirst into the sea to seize their prey in their bills.

Caspian Terns may first draw attention to themselves with their rasping *kraa-ah!* calls. Looking up, you'll be impressed by this large tern. Caspian Terns often throw their weight around, pirating food from other seabirds by frightening them into dropping their hard-earned fish. The Caspians' size is also an advantage when they dive because they can plunge deeper than the smaller terns with whom they tend to associate. Usually only one or two pairs of Caspian Terns will nest among the smaller terns. You'll likely be seeing more of these birds in future since they've become increasingly common in Washington and coastal B.C. It's probably only a matter of time before they will be breeding all the way up to Alaska.

Common Terns migrate along the coast in spring and fall, pausing to snooze on floating logs or kelp beds. In fall they've been spotted in the thousands, diving for small fish such as sandlance or hawking the late summer hatches of flying termites right out of the air.

Common Tern: *breeding*

Seasonal Occurrence & Local Range: *All terns are migratory or summer visitors, and it's always a thrill to see them. Although Arctic Terns are most famous for their arctic to antarctic migrations, they are the least likely of these three terns to be seen because they usually migrate far offshore. However, some breed as far south as the Tatshenshini and Alsek rivers in northwestern B.C.* **Size:** *Caspian: about 53 cm (21 in.); Common and Arctic: about 38 cm (15 in.).*

SWANS

TRUMPETER SWAN
Cygnus buccinator

TUNDRA SWAN
Cygnus columbianus

MUTE SWAN
Cygnus olor

Swans are huge, white waterfowl. Trumpeter Swans resemble Tundras, but their face looks quite different: In the Trumpeter the dark eye blends with the black bill; in the Tundra Swan the eye appears quite separate because of a small yellow patch in front of it. Trumpeters also have a much deeper voice. Mute Swans have an orange-red bill with a bump on top. Young swans are grayish and tough to tell apart.

Trumpeter Swan: *adult*

Swans are the biggest waterfowl in the world, and in truth, they are nothing more, or less, than gigantic, long-necked members of the duck family—a heritage they display in the shapes of their bills. Despite their reputation for beauty and stateliness, these birds can be quite grumpy and quarrelsome, especially when defending their nests.

Even with a good head wind, a big swan needs about five to six meters (20 feet) of takeoff room to become airborne, and the strain on its circulatory system while in flight is such that there is even report of a Whooper Swan in Europe (a close relative of our Trumpeter) dropping out of the sky from a heart attack.

The Tundra Swan is the most widespread member of this group, although it winters mainly in California. However, the Trumpeter is the swan you are most likely to encounter, except in places where the Mute Swan has been introduced from Europe. The Mute Swan is a relatively new arrival, while the Trumpeter is now making a big comeback, as evidenced by increasingly large numbers wintering in fields and open wetlands.

At a distance, you might need a spotting scope to see the bill pattern of some swans and make a positive identification. But remember that it is always a thrill to see a swan—so don't feel bad if you can't identify every single one.

Tundra Swan: *adult*

Mute Swan: *adult*

Seasonal Occurrence & Local Range: *Trumpeters occur along the entire coast, but Mute Swans are found only here and there year-round in southernmost B.C. Tundras winter here but only from the Fraser delta south.*
Size: *Trumpeter and Mute: about 152 cm (60 in.); Tundra: about 135 cm (53 in.).*

CANADA GOOSE
Branta canadensis

Canada Geese have a black head and neck, a broad, white chin strap and a contrasting brown body. Midsized between ducks and swans, geese are at home both on land and in the water. In flight they slice through the skies in V-formations or long lines.

Canada Goose: *adult*

West Coast Canada Geese have enjoyed a recent population explosion thanks to the proliferation of golf courses and city parks, which have lawns where these birds love to graze. Some local populations have become extremely tame, and traffic in park areas can be brought to a halt by casually promenading Canada Geese. In contrast, geese from far-off places are spooky and difficult to approach, and at night in the city, it is a thrill to hear these wild geese migrating.

There are numerous races of Canada Geese, ranging from the Mallard-sized 'cackling' race to giant Canada Geese that may weigh as much as five kilograms (11 pounds). The races mingle in winter on the West Coast, but Canada Geese mate for life and are faithful to their breeding grounds, returning to their birth sites each spring. This clannish tendency keeps the different-sized races of Canada Geese from interpairing since their nesting populations are distinct.

Seasonal Occurrence & Local Range: *Canada Geese are found throughout the area, on both fresh and salt water. They are abundant year-round and even more so in winter, when northern and inland breeders join the locals along the coast.*
Size*: from 64–109 cm (25–43 in.).*

 **SNOW GOOSE**
Chen caerulescens

*Snow-white Snow Geese can be mistaken for
swans, but these geese have shorter necks and
black wing tips. Adults have pink legs, feet
and bill. Immatures are dirty-looking
versions of the adults with dark legs and bill.
The blue phase of the Snow Goose (white
head with dark body and wings) is almost
never seen along the West Coast.*

Snow Goose: *adult*

Each fall in November, Snow Geese arrive in the thousands from Wrangel
Island in Siberia to gorge in the fields and marshes of the Fraser and
Skagit river deltas. Like the Snowy Owl and the Snow Bunting, these
tundra-nesting birds have just the right camouflage color for spring in the
Arctic—plain white.

Instead of flying in well-formed 'V's or straight lines, Snow Geese fly in
wavy lines, yelping noisily. Their call is only vaguely reminiscent of the
familiar honking of their Canada Goose relatives, and to the practiced ear it
is recognizably more musical and usually higher pitched. Their habit of
digging in the mud to feed on rootstocks sometimes stains their heads a
rusty color, and you can't help but feel that it's a shame to smudge such a
handsome bird.

Seasonal Occurrence & Local Range: *This species is mostly a migrant
along the coast from October through April. Its numbers peak in November
and April because many carry on further south to winter.*
Size: *about 71 cm (28 in.).*

DARK MIGRATORY GEESE

BRANT
Branta bernicla

**GREATER WHITE-
FRONTED GOOSE**
Anser albifrons

*Brant are small, all black geese with
a conspicuous white butt and a white
patch on their neck. Greater White-
fronted Geese have a pink bill, a
small white face patch, a gray-
brown body and a white butt.*

Brant: *adult*

Brant are saltwater geese who specialize in eating eelgrass. Their spring
migration routes from Mexico to Alaska look like a dot-to-dot picture,
connecting eelgrass bed to eelgrass bed, and some even detour out to the
Queen Charlotte Islands for a good eelgrass feast.

The world population of Brant plummeted in the 1930s when a blight
decimated the Atlantic Ocean's eelgrass beds. Of necessity, a few Brant
adapted to eating sea lettuce, and eventually the eelgrass beds recovered
along with the Brant. Because the eelgrass beds of the Pacific coast are so
critical to these birds, the urbanization of these areas poses a serious threat
to the species' survival. Many more Brant used to winter along our coast
than do today.

'White-fronts' migrate directly from Alaska to the mouth of the Columbia
before continuing south to California for the winter. It is worth your while
to check all the geese you encounter in hopes of spotting a White-front,
and don't forget to watch for rare blue phase Snow Geese as well.

Seasonal Occurrence & Local Range: *Brant usually are a coastal migrant,
although a few linger over winter and summer from Vancouver Island south,
and in the Queen Charlotte Islands. March through May is a great time for
seeing large numbers of Brant in the Strait of Georgia. In fall Brant fly directly
from Alaska to Baja, missing B.C. and Washington entirely. White-fronts are
most common in southern Washington and Oregon.*
Size: *Brant: about 61 cm (24 in.); Greater White-fronted: about 71 cm (28 in.).*

 **MALLARD**
Anas platyrhynchos

Mallards are the West Coast's most common dabbling duck. The male's iridescent green head and chestnut breast are distinctive. The female's mottled plumage can be confused with other species, but look for the orange and black bill, a white edge along the tail and the white-bordered, blue 'speculum' wing patch in flight.

female

male

Mallard: *adults*

Dabbling ducks (whose scientific names all begin with *Anas*) are well adapted to small bodies of water, hence their other name, 'puddle ducks.' Mallards, the most common of the lot, can spring straight off the water into the air and have no trouble walking on land. This ability, which is shared with all other dabblers, is what makes their puddling ways possible.

Dabblers have a colorful speculum or wing patch. Although males and females of the same species have the same bright speculum, females are generally drab for camouflage on the nest and males colorful for courtship. The males lose their bright plumage after breeding but turn splendid again in the fall. Like all waterbirds, ducks lose all their flight feathers at once and cannot fly until the new ones come in.

Male mallards will sometimes chase female puddle ducks of other species and mate with them against their will. As a result, you may encounter weird and wonderful-looking hybrid ducks that you won't find in this guide or any other.

Seasonal Occurrence & Local Range: *Mallards are found year-round throughout the area. No body of fresh water is too small. Occasionally they are seen on salt water. They are most common in winter, when inland breeders migrate to the milder coast.*
Size: *about 64 cm (25 in.).*

NORTHERN SHOVELER
Anas clypeata

Breeding male Northern Shovelers have a green head, white breast and chestnut flanks; the female is mottled. With its green head, the male shoveler resembles the Mallard; yet the over-sized bill is a give away, as is the light rather than dark breast. At close range the birds' beady, yellow eyes are quite noticeable too. In flight both sexes show a two-tone blue and green forewing.

female

male

Northern Shoveler: *adults*

Northern Shovelers sit low in the water, plowing through floating vegetation and sieving out tasty morsels, or groveling through the muck of bottom ooze. The shovel bill has tiny, comb-like teeth that sort out what the bird will keep and what gets passed through.

Unlike other dabblers, Northern Shovelers rarely tip forward to dabble, although their over-sized bill seems to want to balance them this way. Instead, they stir up the bottom with their feet to bring stuff up to the surface, then sluice through the mud as if panning for gold.

Because of this feeding style, Northern Shovelers prefer quiet, stagnant waters and are often most common on guck-rich sewage ponds.

Seasonal Occurrence & Local Range: *Northern Shovelers are a fairly common year-round resident in this region, breeding on ponds and wintering on both fresh and saltwater marshes and sewage ponds. They are most abundant in spring and fall.*
Size: *about 51 cm (20 in.).*

GADWALL

Anas strepera

The male Gadwall is a mostly gray puddle duck with a black rump and a white wing patch. The female is mottled brown like a female Mallard but has a white belly and a white wing patch.

female
male

Gadwall: *adults*

Because of its almost entirely unspectacular plumage, the Gadwall is a duck you are likely to overlook. Yet the drakes have a charm all their own, and once you learn to recognize them, they stand out in a crowd. As in other more colorful ducks, the plumage pattern of the male Gadwall serves a courtship function, and to a female the black rump and white speculum patch are easily understood signals, especially when the male shows them off to full advantage in pre-nuptial duck dances.

Like many other ducks, the Gadwall is both a migratory bird and a year-round bird. Some come to the coast for the winter from the Interior, and others travel north and south with the seasons. A few Gadwall nest along the coast, although they are not common breeders. They prefer marshes and shallow estuaries, and don't seem to mind brackish water. Gadwalls will dive as well as dabble, and so they don't feed farther from shore than most dabblers.

Hunters used to call Gadwall 'pig ducks' since the male's call is more like a snort than a quack.

Seasonal Occurrence & Range: *This species is found year-round in shallow marshy areas and estuaries throughout our area.*
Size: *about 53 cm (21 in.).*

NORTHERN PINTAIL

Anas acuta

Pintails are elegant, long-necked dabbling ducks. The male's head is chestnut brown with a white line pointing upwards towards the eye. The female is mottled, but her slender shape, long neck and gray bill are distinctive. In flight both sexes show a brown speculum bordered by white on the trailing edge and a pointed, pin-like tail, hence the name acuta.

female

male

Northern Pintail: *adults*

Over a million pintails migrate along the West Coast en route to breeding areas further north. These elegant birds are early migrants and seem anxious to leave and to return as soon as possible. The Fraser River delta and Clayoquot Sound are important staging areas as they push north, and the Fraser estuary is a favorite wintering place.

Each year, new pairs form in late summer or fall. In spring the male follows his new mate to her chosen breeding place on an inland marsh, lake or pond, regardless of where he was born or where he spent the last summer. This breeding strategy ensures mixing of genes and increased diversity in the population.

Occasionally, pintails will nest far from water in a field. You may spot a long neck periscoping above the grass as the duck scans for trouble. As in most duck species, the male waits until the female is on the nest, making sure she is committed to raising her family, before he deserts her and heads off to join the boys for a group bachelor molt in June.

Seasonal Occurrence & Local Range: *Northern Pintails are found throughout the area, but are uncommon in summer. They are abundant in winter when arctic and interior breeding birds return to winter on the mild West Coast.* **Size**: *about 66 cm (26 in.).*

 **WIGEON**

AMERICAN WIGEON
Anas americana

EURASIAN WIGEON
Anas penelope

Male American Wigeon have a white-crowned head with green face patches. Females are gray headed. Both have pinkish-brown sides. Male Eurasian Wigeon have a reddish head, creamy crown and gray sides. Distinguishing female Eurasian Wigeon from their American cousins is very tricky, but in flight the Eurasians show gray wingpits instead of white.

female

male

American Wigeon: *adults*

Male American Wigeon look and sound like old-timers. Their wheezy *wha-ha-ha-ha-ha* sounds like an old geezer laughing at a good joke. And with their white crowns, reminiscent of a balding head, it's no wonder they have been called 'baldpate' by duck hunters.

A leggy duck, wigeon are better walkers than most. Look for these predominantly vegetarian ducks grazing on fallow fields, grassy parks and golf courses. In winter American Wigeon toodle along the upper intertidal zone nibbling at the salty, sea lettuce 'salad bars.'

Since wigeon are restricted to dabbling in shallow waters, they are not above stealing food from coots, who can dive. As soon as the coot pops up from the bottom with a big mouthful of plants, the wigeon snatches the food out of its bill.

Each winter a few Eurasian Wigeon from Siberia and western Alaska infiltrate our local populations; their numbers seem to be on the rise.

Seasonal Occurrence & Local Range: *In winter wigeon are the most abundant dabbling ducks on the west coasts of B.C. and Washington. Although uncommon in summer, they are numerous in winter on fresh water, estuaries, lagoons and shallow bays.*
Size: *both about 61 cm (24 in.).*

TEAL

GREEN-WINGED TEAL
Anas crecca

BLUE-WINGED TEAL
Anas discors

CINNAMON TEAL
Anas cyanoptera

Teal are the smallest of the puddle ducks. Male Green-Winged Teal have an emerald green speculum and a green ear patch on a rich brown head. The female is small and mottled with a green speculum. The male Blue-winged Teal has a blue-gray head with a white crescent moon on its cheek. The male Cinnamon Teal is a uniform glossy copper color, sure to catch your attention. Female Blues and Cinnamons are virtually identical, mottled brown with the same blue speculum as the males.

female · male

Green-winged Teal: *adults*

The pretty, little Green-winged Teal is most abundant here during the winter. Although a few Green-winged Teal breed along the coast, most head further north or inland to their preferred nesting sites on heavily vegetated lakes and ponds.

male

female · male

Blue-winged Teal: *adults*

The bland female could be mistaken for other female dabblers but for her diminutive size and green speculum.

As for the other two species, these little puddle ducks don't mess around with winter on the coast. Come fall, they head straight for Central and South America and don't return until April or May, later than most other ducks. All teal fly fast and low, twisting and turning in perfect precision.

Blue-winged and Cinnamon Teal are not as common as the Green-winged on the coast, but if you do see them, you'll remark on their striking color, small size and powder blue wing patch.

female

male

Cinnamon Teal: *adults*

Seasonal Occurrence & Local Range: *Green-winged Teal range up and down the coast on fresh water; Blue-winged and Cinnamon Teal are more inland birds, uncommon in our area. All three species breed inland; only the Green-winged winters along the coast.*
Size: *all about 38–41 cm (15–16 in.).*

73

SCOTERS

SURF SCOTER
Melanitta perspicillata

WHITE-WINGED SCOTER
Melanitta fusca

BLACK SCOTER
Melanitta nigra

Male scoters are big, black sea ducks; powerful, robust and big billed, they are the Sylvester Stallones of the duck world. The male Surf Scoter has a bold, white square on the back of his head and a swollen, orange-marked bill. White-winged Scoter males are solid black with smallish white wing patches and eye marks; male Black Scoters are plain black with an orange knob on the bill. The plain brown females are trickier, but usually the appropriate females are with their males.

Surf Scoter: *male*

Scoters are tough, diving sea ducks, unruffled by stormy weather. They only move shoreward to hunt for shellfish, which they wrench off the underwater rocks with their sturdy bills before swallowing them whole and grinding them up in their muscular gizzards. One wonders how much of the bluish sand along our coasts, made from pulverized mussel shells, has been processed by the alimentary canals of these ducks.

Surf Scoters are by far the most numerous species of scoter along the coast, but they do associate with the other two species as well. Most often, however, you see large flocks of Surf Scoters hanging out with congregations of Barrow's Goldeneyes. In winter Vancouver's Stanley Park seawall is a terrific place to see scoters. Large numbers overwinter near East Sound in the San Juans too.

Originally called 'scooters,' scoters are named for their habit of scooting across the water before they become airborne. To the more imaginative birder, the wonderful reverberation of their beating wings can be reminiscent of the sound of Arabic women ululating.

White-winged Scoter: *female*

female

male

Black Scoter: *adults*

Seasonal Occurrence & Local Range: *Scoters are seen all along the coast, especially near rich mussel beds. Typically, they are winter residents, although some White-winged Scoters do breed in central B.C. The other two species are arctic breeders; they are predominantly winter waterfowl on the coast, but some nonbreeders are here year-round.*
Size: *all about 51 cm (20 in.).*

HARLEQUIN DUCK

Histrionicus histrionicus

Bold white designer markings on slaty gray and rich chestnut flanks are the striking characteristics of male Harlequin Ducks. The female is drab except for three white patches on her brown head. Don't confuse her with the smaller female Bufflehead, which has only one cheek mark.

male

female

Harlequin Duck: *adults*

Any duck surfing on a frothing stream is almost certainly a Harlequin. White water paddlers have been known to bump into them in midrapid. Baby Harlequins look like fluffy corks totally out of control on the rushing water. Early on, however, these torrent ducks learn to negotiate the currents and dive for the aquatic morsels that make up their diet.

In the spring, pairs of Harlequin Ducks leave the coast to seek out the turbulent fresh waters of mountain rivulets. There they breed and set up a nest in a streamside, hollow stump or rock cavity. As soon as the female starts to incubate, however, the male heads back to the coast, leaving his mate the solo task of raising the young.

Back on the coast, the males band together in large groups to molt. Later on, the females and young join them. In their saltwater phase, Harlequin Ducks are small, spooky sea ducks often seen hunkering down amongst the seaweed on rocky islets or snorkeling in the surge offshore.

Seasonal Occurrence & Local Range: *Harlequins are found all along the coast. They are seen year-round but are most abundant in winter.*
Size: *about 46 cm (18 in.).*

OLDSQUAW
Clangula hyemalis

Although males and females change seasonally, we usually see Oldsquaw in winter garb, when they are piebald with patches of black on a white background. The head, especially, is whiter than in other ducks. The male has a long, quill-like tail almost as long as his body. Both sexes show dark wings in flight.

female

male

Oldsquaw: *winter adults*

These arctic ducks leave their tundra breeding grounds in the fall and lead their young to the rich mussel beds off the Pacific coast.

The call of the Oldsquaw is a loud, three-part yodel: *ah-haa-nah!* The Inuit refer to this bird by simply copying its call, and scientists named it *Clangula hyemalis,* meaning 'noisy winter duck.' Most times you hear Oldsquaw out on the water before you see them. When you do see them, you might wonder why they weren't the ones given the name 'pintail,' since the males' central tail feathers clearly outclass those of the aforementioned puddle duck. The tail is not always visible, however, because they can angle it downwards into the water; but if you do see it, it is unmistakable.

Oldsquaw are terrific divers and can feed at depths of over 60 meters (about 200 feet). They typically show up in northwest waters in November or December, and a few non-breeders hang out in Boundary Bay all summer as well. Orcas Island in the San Juans supports a significant winter population, but these birds do not straggle much further south, even in winter.

Seasonal Occurrence & Local Range: *Oldsquaw can be observed in winter and during spring and fall migration.*
Size: *about 46 cm (18 in.).*

SCAUP AND SIMILAR DUCKS

GREATER SCAUP
Aythya marila

LESSER SCAUP
Aythya affinis

RING-NECKED DUCK
Aythya collaris

TUFTED DUCK
Aythya fuligula

Scaup are like Oreo cookies, dark at both ends and light in the middle. Male Greaters have a rounded, greenish head and Lessers a pointier, purplish head (an iridescence that is often tough to see). Female scaup (the two species are very tough to distinguish) have a white patch at the base of the bill but are otherwise brown. Ring-necked Ducks have a black back, a ringed bill (rather than neck) and a high, angular head. The rare Tufted Duck is similar but with a bit of a ponytail.

male female

Greater Scaup: *adults*

The truth of the matter is that not every scaup can be identified with certainty, although birders love to try. Males at close range are easy; others are downright puzzling. However, Lesser Scaup tend to feed on small, freshwater lakes and ponds, and Greater Scaup frequent big lakes and the ocean.

In winter vast flocks of scaup gather around the Fraser delta and southern Vancouver Island. They are largely nocturnal feeders, so you'll see them snoozing in great numbers during the day in places such as Lost Lagoon, in Vancouver's Stanley Park. In the evening as the sun sets, these ducks stage an impressive changing of the guard. Scaup head out to feed while the Goldeneyes head into the lagoon to sleep, providing a waterfowl spectacle right in the midst of a big city.

Ring-necked Ducks can be seen most commonly on woodland ponds and lakes. They seldom associate with other ducks and are rarely seen on salt water. Tufted Ducks are rare winter visitors that always cause some excitement among birders once they have been located.

male

female

Lesser Scaup: *pair*

Ring-necked duck: *male*

Seasonal Occurrence & Local Range: *All four species can be found at any time of year all along the coast, although they are most common in winter. The Tufted Duck is a rare vagrant from Asia.*
Size: *Greater Scaup: about 51 cm (20 in.); Lesser Scaup, Ring-necked and Tufted Duck: about 43 cm (17 in.).*

CANVASBACK
Aythya valisineria

REDHEAD
Aythya americana

A mahogany head and neck, black breast and pale body are the color patterns of both Canvasback and Redhead males. The Canvasback is larger, with a much lighter back and a 'Roman nose.' Female Canvasbacks have the same profile, but the head is pale brown-gray and washed-out looking. Female Redheads are a bit darker and have a rounder head.

female

male

Canvasback: *adults*

Canvasbacks are a stately duck and larger than most. In the lakes and potholes where they breed, they tend to occupy the central area, diving deeply to forage for plants and aquatic critters on the bottom.

Canvasbacks and Redheads both nest in thick vegetation around shorelines of shallow bodies of water. Redheads are 'egg dumpers' and will lay their eggs in Canvasbacks' nests when they have the chance. Strangely, Redheads do not receive the same scorn that most birders feel for other nest parasites (Brown-headed Cowbirds, for example), probably since most people are happier to see a Redhead than a cowbird, unfair as that may be. In any case, the young Redheads aren't able to out-compete the young Canvasbacks.

Canvasbacks are often seen associating with large mixed flocks of winter waterfowl. The Fraser River delta is the center of their winter abundance along the coast. In contrast, the Redhead is the only duck that winters in larger numbers in the Interior than it does on the coast, where it is relatively rare.

Seasonal Occurrence & Local Range: *These ducks are seen in southern B.C. and occasionally on the Queen Charlottes. They are most abundant during the winter months. A few non-breeders hang around all summer.*
Size: *Canvasback: about 51 cm (20 in.); Redhead: about 46 cm (18 in.).*

BUFFLEHEAD
Bucephala albeola

The Bufflehead is a small duck with a huge, round, black head (actually purplish in the right light) with a large, white wedge in it. The bill is tiny. The duller female has a similar shape, but her head is brown with a white cheek spot, much like a female Harlequin Duck.

male

female

Bufflehead: *adults*

Because Buffleheads have a big head in proportion to their bodies, someone thought they were reminiscent of buffalo and so named them 'buffle' heads. Their big-headed profile is also a clue that they are closely related to goldeneyes. Like their relatives, Buffleheads are also tree hole nesters.

Once mature, the female Bufflehead returns to the area of her birth, where she searches for a cavity, usually a flicker hole, in which to nest. Her small size enables her to squeeze into woodpecker holes only eight centimeters (three inches) wide. Once the last egg is laid, her mate leaves her to incubate and raise the young alone.

Buffleheads explode straight up from the water like tiny, feathered missiles. They will use mountain lakes as breeding sites, and even a beaver pond is large enough for a mother and her young.

These ducks stay in the Interior until late October or November when freeze up forces them to move to the coast.

Seasonal Occurrence & Local Range: *Buffleheads are widely distributed along the coast in winter. They are most common from mid-November to March.*
Size: *about 33 cm (13 in.).*

GOLDENEYES

BARROW'S GOLDENEYE
Bucephala islandica

COMMON GOLDENEYE
Bucephala clangula

Male Barrow's Goldeneye have a white crescent moon on their dark, purplish heads, and white 'finger-marks' on their black flanks. Male Common Goldeneyes have a round, white spot on their dark, greenish cheeks, and all-white flanks. The brown-headed females are trickier: female Barrow's have a steep forehead and, usually, a mostly yellow bill; Commons have a sloping forehead and a mostly dark bill.

female

male

Barrow's Goldeneye: *adults*

The B.C. coast may support as much as 90 percent of the world's population of Barrow's Goldeneyes. These birds often associate with scoters, clustering in huge rafts near rocky shores, where they are easy to observe. Goldeneyes are sometimes called 'whistlers' for the sound of their wings in flight. They dive for mussels and find other tasty invertebrate morsels by rolling over pebbles underwater.

Goldeneyes seem to segregate in the winter. Near Victoria, Common Goldeneyes are abundant and Barrow's are rare. Near Vancouver, Barrow's are much more common.

Despite the similarities between these two species, they don't often get mixed up because they have very distinctive breeding displays that are very entertaining to watch. Goldeneyes court and spark through much of the winter so they don't have to waste time once spring rolls around. Watch the males especially—they will go through an elaborate variety of yoga-like postures and bizarre sounds as they court the females. When they throw their heads way back over their tails, you get a feeling for just how athletic some wild birds can be.

Goldeneyes are tree hole nesters; so, come spring, they head to inland lakes surrounded by cottonwoods and aspens to find the real estate they require. If females fail to find a nest cavity, they spend the summer 'house-hunting' for the next year. Since appropriate tree holes are hard to find, they will use nesting boxes as well.

male female

Common Goldeneye: *adults*

Seasonal Occurrence & Local Range: *Goldeneyes only occasionally breed near the coast. Commons are widely distributed here in winter, but Barrow's are uncommon in the Strait of Juan de Fuca and rare along the west coasts of Washington and Oregon. Densest concentrations occur from mid-November to March.*
Size: *both about 46 cm (18 in.).*

RUDDY DUCK

Oxyura jamaicensis

Ruddy Ducks are easily identified by their small, stout shape and long, stiff tail, often cocked jauntily. The breeding male is a ruddy color with a sky blue bill and a bold white cheek. In winter the male loses his color, but the white cheek remains. The female has the same shape as the male but is mousy brown and has a single line across the cheek.

male

female

Ruddy Duck: *breeding*

Ruddy ducks belong to a group of ducks called 'stiff-tails.' They are the only West Coast representative of this odd, little group. The tail is used as a rudder when swimming and to show off during courtship.

To us, male Ruddy Ducks may appear as charming comedians, but their energetic courtship displays are deadly serious competitions intended to convince the females of their competence as fathers. The males paddle around, beating their breasts with their bright blue beaks, *plap-plap-plap-plap...*, at an ever-increasing speed, until the crescendo is reached: a spasmodic jerk and honking sound.

The preferred habitat of 'Ruddies' is a deep pond or lake bordered by cattails. These ducks sit low in the water and can submerge with nary a ripple. Weak fliers at any time, they usually migrate under the cover of darkness.

Seasonal Occurrence & Local Range: *Ruddies are found in winter from Campbell River southwards on both fresh and salt water. Iona Island, Boundary Bay and Esquimalt Lagoon are good winter sites, as well as Lopez Island in the San Juans. There are only a few breeding sites on Vancouver Island and in the Fraser lowlands.*
Size: *about 38 cm (15 in.).*

WOOD DUCK

Aix sponsa

With its green crested head, white chin strap, scarlet bill and boldly patterned body, a male Wood Duck is an eye-widening sight. The female, though cryptically brown colored, has a touch of class too, with her white Cleopatra eye makeup and crested coiffure.

female   male

Wood Duck: *adults*

It's not surprising that Wood Ducks are favorite subjects for ornamental decoy carvers and others who appreciate the splendor of waterfowl. *Aix sponsa*, the bird's scientific name, says it all—'waterfowl in wedding raiment.'

Although they look like exotic imports, Wood Ducks tend to be locally common on lakes surrounded by deciduous woodland. Seen out of water, these ducks have claws on the tips of their webbed feet to grip branches—an adaptation to their habit of nesting in tree holes, which is, of course, the reason for their common name.

Like many ducks, Wood Ducks change partners each year. The female Wood Duck, however, fiercely defends her nest site from year to year because good tree holes are hard to find and are in high demand by many species of mammals, social wasps and birds, including other ducks.

In the early 1900s, Wood Ducks were threatened with extinction by habitat loss and overhunting. Their numbers have recovered in areas where suitable habitat exists and because they will gladly make use of properly mounted and maintained nest boxes.

Seasonal Occurrence & Local Range: *Wood Ducks are locally common breeders from mid-Vancouver Island south. They occur year-round, with increasingly large overwintering populations on the southern coast of B.C. and in Washington State.*
Size: *about 46 cm (18 in.).*

COMMON MERGANSER
Mergus merganser

Common Mergansers are sleek, elongate ducks with pointy, coral-colored bills. The male has a glossy green head and a mostly white body. The female has a ragged crest and shows a sharp border between the rusty red head and white breast. They are often seen fleeing downriver, their large, white wing patches conspicuous in flight.

female

male

Common Merganser: *adults*

Mergansers are long, lean waterfowl designed for the underwater pursuit of fish. Their bills are saw-like and adapted to slash through the water to grasp and hold fish. If you get close enough, steady your binoculars and you might see the bill's serrated edge.

River runners will know the Common Merganser well, since these ducks are often seen on streams and rivers. The female with her large brood either skulks along the shoreline or patters frantically along the water trying to become airborne. Once these birds are in the air they look jet-like, and fly strongly, low over the water.

Like other tree hole nesters, merganser pairs court in winter so that as soon as areas are ice free they can head inland and get on with raising their brood. The male deserts the female early and rejoins the boys on the coast. It is little wonder that the single females with their large broods often have a harried appearance.

Seasonal Occurrence & Local Range: *Common Mergansers are seen year-round on the coast, but densest concentrations occur from mid-November to March on both salt and fresh water.*
Size: *about 64 cm (25 in.).*

RED-BREASTED MERGANSER
Mergus serrator

Red-breasted Mergansers have the sleek merganser look, but the male's green head is double crested, and he has a white throat, a reddish breast and a black back. The female looks a lot like the female Common Merganser, but there is no sharp border between her rusty head and white body. Red-breasted Mergansers prefer salt water in winter.

Red-breasted Merganser: *male*

'Sawbill' was an old nickname for these birds, and 'sea-robin' was another. Yet it's their punk hairdo that really stands out. It's a good thing the names of birds have been standardized, or who knows what we'd be calling them now.

Red-breasted Mergansers are powerful divers and like to fish in the surge off rocky points. These birds will hunt cooperatively, driving little fish into the shallows. They fish actively, and when they pop up to the water's surface, they maneuver their fish into position before swallowing it, gulping it down headfirst so that the fins don't get stuck. The spiny fin rays of many fish have evolved for exactly this reason, to stick their predators, and you'll sometimes see a fish escape while it's being flipped into place.

In winter these mergansers are more widely distributed along the coast than the other merganser species, and unlike Common Mergansers, they rarely winter inland.

Seasonal Occurrence & Local Range: *Red-breasted Mergansers are common winter visitors from October through April along the coasts of B.C., Washington and Oregon. They are almost never seen here in summer because breeders and nonbreeders alike head to the far north.*
Size: *about 58 cm (23 in.).*

HOODED MERGANSER

Lophodytes cucullatus

A long, thin bill and a large, crested head are characteristic of the Hooded Merganser, the smallest of our mergansers. The male's white crest is bordered in black, and the bird has a complex body pattern with rusty flanks, unlike the Bufflehead, which is mostly white. The female Hooded Merganser has a brown crest and dull black back.

female

male

Hooded Merganser: *adults*

'Hoodies' are delightful little mini-mergansers, although not quite as small as the Smew, a rare vagrant merganser from Asia.

Like Wood Ducks, Hooded Mergansers have a color pattern that seems too elaborate to be believed, and in fact, Hoodies often associate with Wood Ducks. Both are tree cavity nesters. Hoodies have even been known to share incubation with female Wood Ducks and goldeneyes, strange as that may seem.

Since tree holes are a limited resource, immature female Hooded Mergansers begin to search for nesting sites the summer before they breed. Like other ducks, the males leave the females and disappear to molt when their mates start to incubate, after which the sexes rendezvous back on the coast in the fall.

When aroused by danger or passion, the male flares his white head crest, looking about as good as a duck can look.

Seasonal Occurrence & Local Range: *Hoodies are primarily freshwater ducks. They are widely distributed along the coast and up to 1480 meters (about 4800 feet) in elevation. In winter they are most common west of the Cascades and Coast Range from southwest B.C. south through western Oregon.*
Size: *about 46 cm (18 in.).*

AMERICAN COOT
Fulica americana

American Coots are members of the rail family (see page 94) that are frequently mistaken for ducks when swimming. Black with a white frontal shield (a bill that extends up the forehead), they show two white patches under the tail when they tip forward to feed. Coots constantly bob their heads, making them look like windup toys.

American Coot: *adult*

Coots are all-terrain birds—they dabble, dive and walk on land or over floating vegetation. They swim more than other rails, aided by their lobed toes, and can dive to about six meters (about 20 feet). They are equally versatile with respect to the plants they eat and the habitats they frequent, hanging out on ponds, lakes and marshes, and in winter, salt bays and lagoons, or grazing the grass of city parks.

Coots raise their flamboyantly colored young on bodies of water that are surrounded by dense vegetation. Baby coots have a red and blue frontal shield that seems to be a signal to the parents to stuff their little beaks with food.

Dabbling ducks like to wait at the surface and steal the food out of coots' beaks as they emerge, but American Coots are not above doing the same thing to diving ducks such as Canvasbacks, which are even deeper divers.

Seasonal Occurrence & Local Range: *Coots get frozen out of many of their inland haunts in winter and so move to the coast. They prefer fresh water but will occasionally frequent shallow saltwater environments.*
Size: *about 39 cm (15 in.).*

GREAT BLUE HERON ⬛ 🦪 ᵚᵚ 🏔

Ardea herodias

Herons are large, long-legged wading birds with a dagger bill. In flight they hold their long necks in an S-shape. Great Blue Herons are large, gray-blue birds with a cavalier plume of black feathers behind the eye.

Great Blue Heron: *breeding*

Great Blue Herons seem to have too much lift for their skinny bodies. They billow through the air, their broad wings beating slowly. As they fly laboriously to their nests, croaking raucously, they are reminiscent of ancient pterosaurs.

These herons nest colonially with their messy nests of sticks arranged in large trees. The oldest known colony in British Columbia is in Vancouver's Stanley Park, where you can watch the herons' antics through permanent spotting scopes. These rookeries are noisy places (and smelly as well, if you get up close), and while the young are in the nest, they provide some of our best opportunities for watching bird behavior.

Great Blue Herons stand like sentinels, gazing into the water in search of fish, frogs or crabs. They stab their prey with their rapier bills and then struggle to swallow their catch. In winter you'll often see herons standing in fields, mousing.

Seasonal Occurrence & Local Range: *Great Blue Herons remain year-round. If their winter wetlands freeze, they head closer to the coast.*
Size: *about 117 cm (46 in.).*

MEDIUM-SIZED HERONS

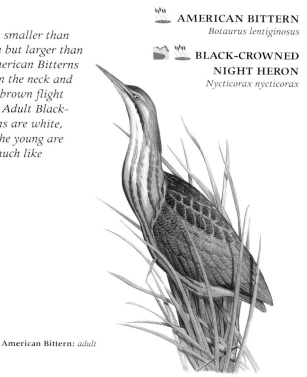

AMERICAN BITTERN
Botaurus lentiginosus

**BLACK-CROWNED
NIGHT HERON**
Nycticorax nycticorax

These two herons are smaller than the Great Blue Heron but larger than the Green Heron. American Bitterns have a black stripe on the neck and blackish rather than brown flight feathers on the wing. Adult Black-crowned Night Herons are white, gray and black, but the young are brown and striped, much like American Bitterns.

American Bittern: *adult*

American Bitterns are more often heard than seen. Their *onk-a-blonk* call sounds like an old water pump being primed, or at least that's what we are told by those who remember such things. These birds move very slowly through their marshy habitats, stopping now and then to grab a fish or other small animal in a sudden darting strike of the bill. When they feel threatened by a potential predator, they adopt the 'bitterning posture,' with the bill pointed to the sky and the body swaying gently like a cattail stem in the breeze.

Black-crowned Night Herons are the least common of the two medium-sized herons in our region, and as their name indicates, they are most active at night. With their stout, heavy bills, they can take prey as large as other birds, especially the nestlings of other marsh species.

Seasonal Occurence & Local Range: *Both species are found in marshes from southern B.C. through coastal Washington and Oregon. American Bitterns are generally solitary, whereas Black-crowned Night Herons are more colonial and much more localized in distribution.*
Size: *both about 58 cm (23 in.).*

91

GREEN HERON

Butorides virescens

This small, dark heron is quite colorful. The neck is a rich chestnut brown; the back and somewhat-crested crown a dark, iridescent blue-green. Also note the short neck, short yellow legs and stout, yellow and black bill.

Green Heron: *adult*

These rather uncommon birds hunt for fish and other small aquatic creatures in dense marshes and along sheltered shorelines. They are slow, methodical hunters and therefore quite secretive, but once spotted, they can often be closely approached.

With their dark backs to camouflage them from airborne predators and their cryptically colored undersides to hide them from their prey, Green Herons are superb stalkers who hunt around the clock. They are especially famous for their ability to use bait to attract fish. A Green Heron will sometimes throw an insect, or even a berry, leaf or twig, on the water and wait for curious fish to come by to examine the lure. Technically, this behavior is a sort of tool-use, but it is the result of a wonderful evolutionary adaptation, not a great deal of intelligence.

The range of this species has been slowly expanding in the West Coast area and the herons can be found here year-round. After breeding, they tend to disperse in search of food, after which some, but not all, of the population migrates south for the winter.

Seasonal Occurrence & Range: *Green Herons are found from southern Vancouver Island and the Lower Mainland south through Washington. Some overwinter, but most sightings occur in spring and summer.*
Size: *about 43 cm (17 in.).*

SANDHILL CRANE

Grus canadensis

Sandhill Cranes are very tall, long-legged, solid gray birds with a naked, red crown. They fly with neck outstretched, often gliding and soaring rather than continually flapping. You almost always hear their strange gruu-ing calls, as they fly high overhead, long before you see the birds themselves.

Sandhill Crane: *adult*

Cranes are more closely related to rails than to the similar-looking herons, but they can be distinguished by their outstretched neck in flight. Cranes also have a bustle of feathers on the rump, which the other groups lack, but you are not likely to notice it unless the bird is standing.

Crane populations have suffered seriously owing to the loss of their wetland habitats, but the Sandhill Crane is still doing much better than its close relative the Whooping Crane (not found on the West Coast), of which only a few hundred remain.

Although never abundant on the coast, Sandhill Cranes are a thrill to see, whether in the air or on the ground in an open field. In spring in the Queen Charlottes, you may spot a pair of these tall, gray birds feeding on tidal flats or searching for a nest site in remote bogs. A few pairs still nest in the Burns Bog and Pitt Meadows areas of southern B.C.

Cranes mate for life, reinforcing their pair bond each year with an elaborate mating dance. It has often been equated with human dancing, but the comparison seems forced until you see the real thing. Only the right dance steps, by each bird in turn, will take them to the next step in their courtship.

Seasonal Occurrence & Local Range: *The Sandhill Crane is not a common West Coast bird. Generally, it is seen only on migration, more commonly in fall than in spring. A few breed in the Queen Charlottes and the southern B.C. Mainland.*
Size: *about 104 cm (41 in.).*

RAILS

VIRGINIA RAIL
Rallus limicola

SORA
Porzana carolina

Rails are more often heard than seen. Virginia Rails have a deliberate wraak, wrak, wrak, wrak *call, whereas Soras call* sore-rah! sore-rah! *or give a loud descending whinny. Virginia Rails have a long red bill, gray cheeks and rusty breast. Soras have a short yellow bill, black face and gray neck.*

Virginia Rail: *adult*

Virginia Rails and Soras live hidden lives, deep in marshy vegetation. Their bodies, compressed side-to-side, are perfectly designed for slipping between rushes, hence the expression 'thin as a rail.' Their long toes keep them afloat on the mud, and they seldom swim, although they can.

Their loud voices fill the air during the day and join the evening chorus in the marsh. A good way to see rails is to play a recording of their call back to them. Ever territorial, they will cautiously investigate the intruder, nervously flicking their tails and twisting their heads as they step gingerly with their oversized feet. (But don't overdo it, and remember not to use tapes in places where birdwatchers congregate.) Another good way to see them is to don chest waders, sit down in the marsh, and wait for them to pass by.

Rails lay large clutches of eggs that are tended by both parents. The young are precocious and start feeding themselves as soon as they hatch.

Sora: *breeding*

Seasonal Occurrence & Local Range: *Virginia Rails both breed and winter in coastal wetlands from southern B.C. southwards. Soras are summer residents, from April to September.*
Size: *Virginia Rail: about 23 cm (9 in.); Sora: about 20 cm (8 in.).*

BLACK OYSTERCATCHER
Haematopus bachmani

Black Oystercatchers are crow-sized, black wading birds with a long, red bill and flesh-colored legs. One friend says they look like a crow smoking a carrot. Their button-like, yellow eyes are outlined with red, and the overall impression of this bird is just plain comical. Look for them on rocky islands and shores.

Black Oystercatcher: *adult*

Black Oystercatchers always sound upset. Their high, continuous call is often the first clue that they are around. You may spot their fluttery flight low to the water or see them poking about for food in the intertidal zone of rocky shores. Despite their flamboyant red bills, they blend in amazingly well as they search for limpets and mussels, but usually not oysters. Since they whack their food off the rocks and then chisel it open with their bill, thinner-shelled menu items are preferred.

Young Black Oystercatchers learn from their parents how to open their hard-shelled foods. Since this foraging style requires skill, the young often stay with their parents up to a year, in order to get fed while they refine their techniques. If they survive the early perils, these birds may live over 30 years.

Black Oystercatchers are most common on rocky shores, where they lay their eggs in minimalist nests on exposed rocks. Crows and ravens take their toll, so the oystercatchers' strategy is simply to lay another batch, which they may do as many as five times in a season.

Seasonal Occurrence & Local Range: *Black Oystercatchers are found all along the coast where the shores are rocky and rich in intertidal life. They are year-round residents.*
Size: *about 43 cm (17 in.).*

 # REGULAR PLOVERS

BLACK-BELLIED PLOVER
Pluvialis squatarola

AMERICAN GOLDEN-PLOVER
Pluvialis dominicus

PACIFIC GOLDEN-PLOVER
Pluvialis fulva

In breeding plumage, Black-bellied Plovers have a distinctive black face and belly. In winter they turn a dull, specked gray, and in any plumage they have distinctive black wingpits. American Golden-Plovers and Pacific Golden-Plovers are difficult to distinguish from one another; they are black and gold where Black-bellied Plovers are black and white.

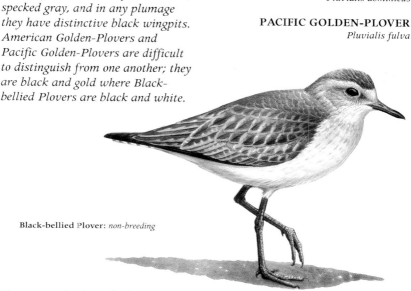

Black-bellied Plover: *non-breeding*

Plovers are thick-necked, medium-sized shorebirds with a short bill on a squarish head. They have an upright posture and tend to run in short bursts.

Black-bellied Plovers breed in the Arctic and winter from southern B.C. south to Chile. They feed on mud flats, sandy shores and in wet fields. Boundary Bay near Vancouver, B.C. and the Oak Bay golf course, close to Victoria, B.C., are two good bets for winter sightings.

Black-bellied Plovers defend winter feeding territories, and if food resources are limited, they become very aggressive with other birds. They tend to spread out along the beach to feed; nevertheless, their plaintive cries of *pee-u-wee* serve to keep their flocks loosely together. They often associate with other plovers, and turnstones too. Occasionally, you may spot American Golden-Plovers or Pacific Golden-Plovers hanging out with Black-bellied Plovers on migration.

Seasonal Occurrence & Local Range: *Black-bellied Plovers are most likely to be seen during migration, but they are locally common in winter. American or Pacific Golden-Plovers are seen here only when migrating.*
Size: *all about 28 cm (11 in.).*

RING-NECKED PLOVERS

KILLDEER
Charadrius vociferus

SEMIPALMATED PLOVER
Charadrius semipalmatus

Killdeer are easily identified as the plover with two bold breast bands. In flight or when alarmed, they flash a rusty rump. Killdeer are named for their call, kill-dee! kill-dee!
Semipalmated Plovers are smaller and have a single, narrow breast band and a back-tipped, orange bill.

Killdeer: *adult*

Killdeer are landlubbers. They have adapted well to urbanization, spreading far beyond coastal shores to golf courses, playing fields, farms and old industrial sites. Despite their bold markings, Killdeer are remarkably well camouflaged and rely on their near invisibility, laying their eggs virtually out in the open. The pebble-colored eggs are deposited directly on the ground. If you wander near their nest site, however, they try to lure you away by crying pitifully and feigning a broken wing. Their Latin name *vociferus* aptly describes this vocal bird.

Semipalmated Plovers are more often seen at the beach. When the tide is high, they snooze, waiting for the waters to expose the wet sand. Then they run about looking for crustaceans and worms, all the while avoiding the lapping waves on fleet feet, which are partly webbed, hence the name 'semipalmated.'

Seasonal Occurrence & Local Range: *Killdeer are common year-round residents. Semipalmated Plovers are most common in migration in April and May and again in July and August.*
Size: *Killdeer: about 25 cm (10 in.); Semipalmated Plover: about 18 cm (7 in.).*

COMMON SNIPE
Gallinago gallinago

An extremely long bill, plump body, striped head and rich brown on buff plumage distinguish this species. Snipe are secretive loners, whereas dowitchers, with which they could be confused, tend to be gregarious. 'Snipes have stripes,' but dowitchers look evenly brown or gray.

Common Snipe: *adult*

Common Snipe are extremely confident in their camouflage, allowing you to approach very near until they explode into zigzag flight. This fallback strategy, accompanied by sharp *scaip!* calls, is fairly effective, usually enabling them to elude predators or gunshot. Consequently, these snipe were once considered a good game bird by hunters.

The winnowing sound of a Common Snipe's territorial display is a quavering *huh-huh-huh-huh* sound that you feel as much as hear, often late at night. The eerie sound is produced as the bird makes shallow dives in its territorial flight and the air whistles through its outer tail feathers. For most people, the discovery that the Common Snipe's most characteristic sound is not a vocalization at all is one of the primary, nifty facts of the outdoors.

The Common Snipes' long, flexible bill is an able tool for probing the mud of the soggy meadows and bogs where they live, and they feed themselves on small invertebrates pulled from deep within the substrate.

Seasonal Occurrence & Local Range: *Common Snipe are year-round residents where the wet ground remains unfrozen.*
Size: *about 28 cm (11 in.).*

YELLOWLEGS

GREATER YELLOWLEGS
Tringa melanoleuca

LESSER YELLOWLEGS
Tringa flavipes

Yellowlegs are slender, mottled, gray-brown shorebirds. In flight their white rump is exposed and their long legs dangle. Greater Yellowlegs are larger with a longer, ever-so-slightly upturned bill with a pale base. Lesser Yellowlegs are medium sized with a straight, all-dark bill. They have a one- or two-note chew-chew *call; the Greater Yellowlegs' call consists of three to five* chews.

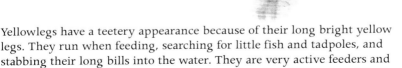

Greater Yellowlegs: *breeding*

Lesser Yellowlegs: *breeding*

Yellowlegs have a teetery appearance because of their long bright yellow legs. They run when feeding, searching for little fish and tadpoles, and stabbing their long bills into the water. They are very active feeders and will often wade as deeply as possible, sweeping their bill back and forth just below the water's surface. Sometimes they forage cooperatively, forming a line and driving their prey into shallow water.

Greater Yellowlegs often associate with Lesser Yellowlegs and other medium-sized waders, and these gatherings give beginning birdwatchers a fine opportunity to compare these almost identically patterned birds. Once you get the hang of recognizing them by their shape and the look in their eye, you will soon find that much of birding is based on these sorts of features rather than color or pattern.

Seasonal Occurrence & Local Range: *Yellowlegs are more common inland than along the coast. Greater Yellowlegs breed in interior B.C. and are commonly seen on the coast in migration. Some regularly winter west of the Cascades. Lesser Yellowlegs are most commonly seen in fall migration, although they do not linger long.*
Size: *Greater: about 36 cm (14 in.); Lesser: about 25 cm (10 in.).*

SOLITARY SANDPIPER

Tringa solitaria

The Solitary is a medium-sized sandpiper with a white eye-ring and medium-length, greenish-yellow legs. It is brown and speckled above, white breasted below and has a habit of bobbing intermittently and extending its wings above its back when it lands.

Solitary Sandpiper: *breeding*

Although not common, the Solitary Sandpiper does show up on migration. This species' relatedness to the yellowlegs is evident in its looks and occasional bobbing behavior. Preferring fresh water to the seashore, it is a denizen of small waterbodies and often hangs out near puddles and farm-yards, usually alone. To distinguish Solitary Sandpipers from yellowlegs, look for the prominent white eye-ring, dull-colored legs and lack of a white rump patch in flight.

Solitary Sandpipers breed in boggy areas east of the Coast Ranges, where they seek out old nests (often situated in conifers) of robins, waxwings and blackbirds. In these areas, when you see an irritated shorebird perched high on a black spruce, it almost always turns out to be a Solitary Sandpiper— scolding the birder for entering its nesting territory.

Seasonal Occurrence & Local Range: *Solitary Sandpipers pass through in spring and fall.*
Size: *about 20 cm (8 in.).*

PHALAROPES

RED-NECKED PHALAROPE
Phalaropus lobatus

WILSON'S PHALAROPE
Phalaropus tricolor

RED PHALAROPE
Phalaropus fulicaria

Red-necked Phalaropes in non-breeding plumage are gray above and white below and have a strong dark line through the eye. The breeding plumage of females shows a dark, rufous patch on the neck framing a white chin; the male is similar but paler. Wilson's Phalaropes have a longer, thinner, black bill; a black line through the eye; and in summer, a bar of red color down the neck. Rarely seen, Red Phalaropes in winter plumage are pale gray above and white below, with a small, dark patch through the eye.

Red-necked Phalarope: *breeding male*

Phalaropes are small, dainty, sandpiper-like birds with very thin bills, usually seen swimming erratically on the water or spinning in circles. Pirouetting, they stir up plankton with their lobed toes and stitch the water with their beaks to pick it up. Although this behavior looks like the equivalent to patting your head while rubbing your belly, it seems to work for these birds.

Females wear the bright colors in this group. They are typically larger than the males and eschew all the familial duties of incubation and rearing their young.

Only the Wilson's Phalarope, which breeds east of the Cascades and Coast Mountains, is likely to be seen walking since the other two species breed in the far north and tend to migrate offshore.

Phalarope numbers are somewhat erratic, varying from year to year, depending on food availability, we presume.

Wilson's Phalarope: *breeding female*

Seasonal Occurrence & Local Range: *Red-necked Phalaropes are common migrants. On the West Coast they are seen most often in fall, particularly in the San Juans, Georgia Strait and off the shore of southern Vancouver Island. Wilson's Phalaropes are seen in May and June. Red Phalaropes are rarely seen because they migrate offshore.*
Size: *all about 20 cm (8 in.).*

DOWITCHERS

LONG-BILLED DOWITCHER
Limnodromus scolopaceus

SHORT-BILLED DOWITCHER
Limnodromus griseus

Dowitchers are long-billed, chunky shorebirds, usually seen in groups. In flight they show a wedge of white on their backs. It's easiest to separate them by call. Keek! *is the note of the Long-billed, and a* tu-tu-tu *sound, reminiscent of a watch alarm, is that of the Short-billed.*

Short-billed Dowitcher: *non-breeding*

Dowitchers cluster in tight groups up to their bellies in the water. In their zeal, they will completely submerge their heads as they stitch the mud with their long bills, working like sewing machines on high speed. Even when resting, dowitchers stick close together—it's rare to see one on its own.

Dowitchers frequent mud flats, where mucking about turns up adequate food. They will check out farm ponds and muddy fields too. Experts say that Short-billeds favor saltwater habitats and Long-billeds prefer fresh water, but since they are so hard to distinguish, it's best not to identify them on habitat alone. The calls of the two species are a better clue. Listen to a recording or, better yet, take one out birding with you so you can compare the sound of a 'known' dowitcher to the one you are watching at the time.

Seasonal Occurrence & Local Range: *Dowitchers breed in the high north and winter from the southern states through South America, so we see them mostly in migration—more frequently heading south (mid-July through October) than north (April to May). Overwintering birds are typically Long-billed; Short-billed Dowitchers are rare after September.*
Size: *both about 28 cm (11 in.).*

 **WESTERN SANDPIPER**
Calidris mauri

The Western Sandpiper is a 'peep,' a generic term for a group of small, grayish sandpipers that look and act a lot alike. The Western has black legs and a longish, slightly drooping bill. Smart rufous edges to feathers on its back are especially obvious in breeding plumage.

Western Sandpiper: *breeding*

In late April the mud flats of the West Coast resemble a lumpy, rusty carpet as most of the world's population of Western Sandpipers stops to feed en route to the species' breeding grounds in Siberia and northern Alaska. The birds make short hops along the coast, touching down to refuel at San Francisco Bay, Gray's Harbor on the Washington coast, the Fraser delta and then the mouths of the Stikine and Copper rivers.

These feeding areas are essential for them to gorge on abundant food for several days and pack on the fat. But these sandpipers require just the right amount of fat. Too much fat slows them down and makes them an easier target for fast-flying falcons. Too little fat and a sandpiper will run out of energy before the next feeding ground.

Fat reserves alone are not enough to fuel the birds for the next leg of their migration. Western Sandpipers require favorable tails winds to help blow them north. These 'wind birds' migrate between 1000 and 3000 meters high (3000–10,000 feet), surfing on jet streams of about 50 km/hr. (30 mi./hr.).

Seasonal Occurrence & Local Range: *Migrants are much more abundant in April and May as they pass through en route to Alaska. Fall migrants show up in June through September—first the adults still in breeding plumage, then the juveniles.*
Size: *about 15 cm (6 in.).*

105

LEAST SANDPIPER
Calidris minutilla

SEMIPALMATED SANDPIPER
Calidris pusilla

Yellowish legs distinguish the Least Sandpiper; also, it appears smaller and darker brown than other peeps, and its short, thin bill is very slightly downcurved. The Semipalmated Sandpiper is slightly larger with black legs and a shorter, straighter bill than the Least or Western Sandpiper.

Least Sandpiper: *non-breeding*

Peeps are gregarious birds seen flying in tight, wheeling flocks or speedily twiddling along coastal flats probing the sand or mud with sewing machine-like stitches of their long bills.

As both its names suggest, the Least Sandpiper is the smallest North American shorebird, although comparisons can be difficult when sandpipers are spread out, running down a beach. Although the yellow legs are a good field mark, bad light or legs caked with mud can confuse matters.

Least Sandpipers feed high on the beach at the upper edge of mud flats, on seashores and inland ponds. They often run in a hunched position, stopping to peck or probe the sand.

Semipalmated Sandpipers are hard to distinguish from Leasts and Westerns, but the Westerns' longer bill enables them to probe farther out on the mud flats than the look-alike Semipalmated and Least Sandpipers, who join them at local mud bars.

Speedy feeders, Semipalmateds scurry along the beach on their partially webbed (semipalmated) toes, stopping to pick at morsels of food; then off they race once more.

When all else fails, the catchall name of peeps comes in handy and corresponds roughly to these birds' generic name *Calidris*. Even when identification is impossible, it is still a pleasure to watch them flying in air show formations and dashing down the beach.

Semipalmated Sandpiper: *non-breeding*

Seasonal Occurrence & Local Range: *Least Sandpipers are abundant along the Washington and B.C. coast in April and May, and again from late July through September. Occasionally a few overwinter. More Semipalmateds pass through in fall than in spring, although in nowhere near the numbers of their close brethren the Westerns and Leasts.*
Size: *Least: about 13 cm (5 in.); Semipalmated: about 15 cm (6 in.).*

SANDERLING
Calidris alba

The Sanderling is a medium-sized peep. Winter birds are pale gray with black shoulders. Their bills are short and straight, and their legs are black. Immatures are spangled with black and buff above. Breeding birds are orangish flecked with black on their breast and upper parts.

Sanderling: *non-breeding*

Sanderlings are charming beach walking companions. They sprint ahead of advancing waves, then charge after them as they retreat, gobbling up food on the most recently exposed surfaces of sandy beaches.

Their Latin name, *alba*, means 'white,' and these sandpipers in winter plumage can look ghostly as they forage at night on moonlit beaches. Other times they can be seen perched on floating beds of kelp, picking at tender tidbits such as tiny crustaceans called amphipods.

When resting, Sanderlings tuck one leg up to preserve their body heat. They will remain resolutely one legged, hopping ahead of an approaching beach walker, evoking unsolicited sympathy and concern. Sometimes the sight of an entire flock of apparently one-legged birds helps you clue in to the fact that their one leggedness is simply a behavioral quirk.

Seasonal Occurrence & Local Range: *Sanderlings are common migrants and abundant winter visitors to sandy coastal beaches from British Columbia south. They are especially abundant on the south coasts of Washington and northern Oregon. Sanderlings depart in late April for their high arctic breeding grounds.*
Size: *about 20 cm (8 in.).*

DUNLIN
Calidris alpina

Dunlin are short-necked, medium-sized sandpipers with a long, thick bill that droops at the tip. In spring Dunlin trade their somber, winter grays for cinnamon reds on their back, and a bold black belly.

Dunlin: *non-breeding*

Dunlin are the most common overwintering shorebird of the West Coast. While most shorebirds start passing through in late summer and then carry on much further south, Dunlin don't arrive from their northern tundra breeding grounds until late October. Then they radiate into a wide variety of habitats, including gravel and sand beaches, as well as protected coastlines and flooded fields. But mud flats, where they feast on crustaceans, are by far their favorites.

These areas are also home to many birds of prey. Safety in numbers is the Dunlin's style, and as a Peregrine Falcon flies in for the kill, the group wheels in a bewildering aerial ballet, flashing light and dark patterns like venetian blinds.

In winter, with low tides at night, Dunlin often just hang out and rest during the day, keeping one eye cocked for danger.

Seasonal Occurrence & Local Range: *Most Dunlin disappear to breed in the tundra around mid-May and return in October. Occasionally, a few stick around all summer.*
Size: *about 20 cm (8 in.).*

PECTORAL SANDPIPER
Calidris melanotos

The Pectoral Sandpiper is a medium-sized sandpiper. It is small headed and full breasted, with heavy, brownish breast streaks ending in a sharp line above the white belly. These birds have greenish-yellow legs.

Pectoral Sandpiper: *breeding*

Their big-chested appearance with a neat dividing line between the brown and white areas make Pectoral Sandpipers easy to identify—an unusual pleasure when you are dealing with shorebirds. In fact, they are distinctive enough that few birdwatchers think of them as a true peep, despite their membership in the genus *Calidris*.

Pectoral Sandpipers are locally common fall migrants with a habit of feeding in wet fields and puddles, which has led to some birders calling them 'grass snipes.' When disturbed, they stop feeding and crane their necks above the grass to assess any potential danger. They often feed well spread out, but if frightened, they take flight and quickly form a small flock.

Where small groups have gathered, the males are visibly larger than the females, although their markings are the same.

Seasonal Occurrence & Local Range: *Pectoral Sandpipers pass through in spring but are seen more commonly from July through October.*
Size: *about 22 cm (8.5 in.).*

 **SPOTTED SANDPIPER**
Actitis macularia

Spotted Sandpipers are small with a spotty breast (in summer). They have a high, plaintive peet-weet-weet *call and a stiff-winged, arthritic flight interspersed with glides. As they land, they teeter vigorously, and bob as they walk along the shore. 'Spotties' are often seen on fresh water.*

Spotted Sandpiper: *breeding*

Spotted Sandpipers are the most widespread shorebird in freshwater environments, although they may also show up by the sea, especially in winter or on migration. These little birds are wide ranging, from sea level to the alpine, and occur all over North America. In many parts of the continent they are the only sandpiper to be found. In other places they occur alongside a myriad of similarly sized peeps, but their 'tipsy-teapot' behavior makes them relatively easy to identify.

Mother Spotties are the fast-living females of the bird world, starting families with as many as five males per season. They compete for males in the spring, reversing the usual order of things among birds. Once a nest is set up and the eggs are laid, the female leaves her mate to raise the family and sets up house with another male elsewhere. Only the last male in her summer series is blessed with her help in raising the young.

Seasonal Occurrence & Local Range: *Spotted Sandpipers are seen wherever there is water with adjacent vegetation—freshwater habitats in summer, coastal habitats in winter. They are most common in summer.*
Size: *about 19 cm (7.5 in.).*

SANDPIPERS OF
ROCKY COASTS

SURFBIRD
Aphriza virgata

ROCK SANDPIPER
Calidris ptilocnemis

These two species are often seen on surf-washed rocks. Surfbirds are stocky with a short bill that is yellow at the base of the lower mandible. In winter plumage they are plain gray and white; the tail is white at the base and dark at the tip. In breeding plumage they are speckled black and white with rufous shoulders. Rock Sandpipers are smaller, with a slightly droopy, medium-long bill and short, green-yellow legs.

Surfbird: *non-breeding*

A kayaker squints at an offshore reef. The black rocks appear to be moving. Surfbirds in a dense flock scamper amidst the surging waves, prying off acorn barnacles with their short, plover-like beaks. They live up to their names, scarcely pausing as waves crash around them and sometimes over them.

Surfbirds are confused sometimes with the slightly smaller and darker turnstones with which they often associate.

Then again, a flicker-like whistling from a flock of shorebirds on a rocky reef could reveal a Rock Sandpiper, a less commonly seen 'rockpiper' that hangs out with Surfbirds, turnstones and tattlers.

Rock Sandpipers resemble Dunlin in spring and summer, but the Rock Sandpipers' habitat and their pale legs are telling.

Seasonal Occurrence & Local Range: *Surfbirds are locally common migrants and winter visitors. They breed in rocky alpine areas in Alaska and the Yukon. Less common, Rock Sandpipers winter from October to May on rocky shores.*
Size: *Surfbird: about 25 cm (10 in.); Rock Sandpiper: about 20 cm (8 in.).*

RED KNOT

Calidris canutus

These stout, green-legged shorebirds look a lot like big, fat Sanderlings. In breeding plumage they have robin-red underparts; in winter they are gray on the back with white underparts.

Red Knot: *breeding*

Like so many other shorebirds, Red Knots breed in the High Arctic and winter in South America. Their migration flights are long and usually swift, sometimes covering a thousand miles in a single day. However, they do stop to 'fuel up' at traditional staging areas. In spring the only such areas for Red Knots in our region are Gray's Harbor and Willapa Bay in Washington. Outside these hot spots, this species is rare. Shorebird biologists have identified a number of such key staging areas along the Red Knots' route, and protection of these spots should ensure the viability of shorebird migrations into the future.

When feeding, the birds focus in on mollusks, other marine invertebrates and even small fishes, although they probe in the mud for most of their food, after the fashion of other 'peep' shorebirds, to which they are closely related.

Apparently, the Red Knot was once the most common shorebird in North America, and although its numbers appear to be strong at present, it is still an uncommon sight in our area. Where 'our' Red Knots go to breed and to winter is still an unsolved mystery.

Seasonal Occurrence & Range: *Red Knots are seen here and there along the coast, especially during the prolonged fall migration, except for spring concentrations at Gray's Harbor and Willapa Bay, Washington.*
Size: *about 27 cm (10.5 in.).*

TURNSTONES

BLACK TURNSTONE
Arenaria melanocephala

RUDDY TURNSTONE
Arenaria interpres

Turnstones are stocky shorebirds with a medium-length, sharp bill flattened at the base. In winter Black Turnstones have a black head and breast, the black ending in a straight line above the white belly. They show a bold black and white pattern in flight. Ruddy Turnstones have orange legs rather than black, and in winter more white, splotchy patches on the head. In breeding season they show a rusty 'calico' back.

Black Turnstone: *non-breeding*

Black Turnstones are the most common rockpiper of rocky outer shores and frequently associate with Surfbirds. Peering intently at the rocks, these turnstones flip over shells and 'leave no stone unturned' in their constant quest for fresh seafood. If startled from their preoccupation, they explode into flight, flashing their bold flight markings and chattering noisily in alarmed indignation.

The Black Turnstone's flamboyant ruddy relatives are seen less often, but occur in a greater variety of habitats. Ruddy Turnstones pause in migration on rocky or sandy shores, or pebble beaches, and both their gorgeous calico cat colors and foraging styles are attention getting. They industriously flip stones on cobble beaches, scavenge insects and excavate big holes in sandy beaches.

Seasonal Occurrence & Local Range: *Black Turnstones are numerous outside of the breeding season, from late July through to spring. Ruddy Turnstones are usually only seen in spring and fall migration.*
Size: *both about 23 cm (9 in.).*

WANDERING TATTLER

Heteroscelus incanus

This bird has a long, straight bill and a dark line through the eye with a light line above; its plumage is plain gray above, always. It shows a gray breast with a white belly in winter and a barred breast and belly in summer. Like the Spotted Sandpiper, the Wandering Tattler often teeters.

Wandering Tattler: *non-breeding*

Human beachcombers often look up to see a conservative-looking, gray shorebird walking on rocks at the water's edge; like many beach walkers, the Wandering Tattler seems to enjoy solitude. Approach too closely and the tattler will fly away with a loud, ringing *twheee-twee-twee* call, 'tat-tling' a warning. Its large size and teetering walk immediately identify it as a Wandering Tattler.

These birds are indeed great wanderers, ranging in winter down the coast of South America and sometimes island hopping across the South Pacific as far as Australia. Winter holidays in Hawaii are often sprinkled with sightings of the Wandering Tattler.

This shorebird is another species that will become familiar to birdwatchers by its overall look. Serious birdwatchers call this look the 'jizz' of a bird, a term that originated in the military and referred to the general impression, size and shape of an unidentified aircraft. Why the word isn't spelled 'giss' is simply one more annoying inconsistency in the language of birdwatching and bird names.

Seasonal Occurrence & Local Range: *Wandering Tattlers occasionally are seen in spring but more commonly in late summer and early fall when they migrate along the coast from their northern breeding grounds.*
Size: *about 29 cm (11.5 in.).*

WHIMBREL
Numenius phaeopus

With its long, decurved bill and prominent head stripes, the Whimbrel is as distinctive as a large, plain, brown shorebird can be.

Whimbrel: *adult*

Formerly called the Hudsonian Curlew, the Whimbrel shares the scimitar-shaped bill and plaintive call of its curlew relatives, along with member-ship in the curlew genus *Numenius.*

The sight of one of these large, impressive shorebirds connects you with the wild ways of nature. The West Coast is just one stop along the way for these wandering creatures. Powerful fliers, Whimbrels strike out across the open ocean, sometimes pausing in such far-flung places as the Ecuadorian Galapagos and in Canada's equivalent, the Queen Charlottes, en route to their arctic breeding grounds.

Over land, Whimbrels fly high in the sky, sometimes in V-formations. Pausing to feed, they tweeze deeply into the mud, plucking small crabs from their burrows. They may also feed in salt marshes and on sand dunes, picking prey from the surface as well as probing.

Seasonal Occurrence & Local Range: *Although Whimbrels have been sighted every month of the year, they are seen most often in April through May, and then in late June through October.*
Size: *about 43 cm (17 in.).*

RING-NECKED PHEASANT

Phasianus colchicus

Ring-necked Pheasants, especially the mottled brown females, look like long-tailed chickens. The males are spectacularly multicolored, with a glossy green head, red face and white necklace above bronzed body feathers. Up close, the complexity of this plumage is astonishing.

Ring-necked Pheasant: *male*

When flushed, Ring-necked Pheasants rise with a loud *awk-ock!* and a frantic flapping of wings, gliding away to a new hiding place in a brushy thicket. At other times they can be seen striding through fields with all the pomp of a visiting dignitary, which in a sense they are. Ring-necked Pheasants were introduced to North America from China in the late 1800s, originally in Oregon, for the purpose of sport hunting. Since then, they have been released many times at many places in the region, as they are easy to breed in captivity.

These pheasants have adapted well to agricultural lands and fields of all types, providing they have brushy areas in which to hide. In spring the male finds a conspicuous perch and crows to attract his harem of females. The females are casual parents and lay large numbers of eggs to compensate for inevitable losses.

In recent years loss of brushy areas to urbanization and removal of brush in farming areas have taken their toll. Once common, Ring-necked Pheasants have become rare in places such as the San Juans.

Seasonal Occurrence & Local Range: *Ring-necked Pheasants occur year-round in the southern coastal areas of B.C., and Washington and Oregon.*
Size: *Male: about 84 cm (33 in.); Female: about 53 cm (21 in.).*

117

RUFFED GROUSE 🌲 🏔

Bonasa umbellus

Grouse are chicken-sized, ground-dwelling birds. Both male and female Ruffed Grouse have a brown camouflage pattern and a crested head. When displaying, the male fans his tail, showing a dark subterminal band, and can extend black ruffs on the sides of his neck.

Ruffed Grouse: *male*

When a male Ruffed Grouse is displaying somewhere nearby, he makes a sound you feel more than hear, as a forest drum beat reverberates in your chest. The grouse struts on a log, and with tail fanned and neck ruffed, he beats the air with accelerating wing strokes to proclaim his territory.

A female Ruffed Grouse may respond to the advertisement and home in. If she is satisfied that the male is a fit father, she mates with him, and there the relationship ends. Fortunately, young grouse are precocious and do not rely on two parents to feed them. Almost as soon as the chicks hatch, they are up and running after their mother, following her example of pecking at insects, buds and leaves.

Birds such as grouse, which do not provide much parental care, tend to have large numbers of young to compensate for the increased likelihood of losing some chicks along the way. This strategy may seem harsh, but birds in general produce nowhere near the extreme numbers of offspring seen in most species of fishes, reptiles and amphibians.

Seasonal Occurrence & Local Range: *Ruffed Grouse are year-round residents in mixed forests from sea level to about 2000 meters (about 6500 feet). They are not found in the Queen Charlottes or the San Juans.*
Size: *about 40 cm (16 in.).*

BLUE GROUSE
Dendragapus obscurus

The Blue Grouse is a large grouse. Males are uniformly charcoal colored, with a pale gray band on a dark tail and yellow-orange comb above the eye. Similar to the Ruffed Grouse, the female is mottled brown but has a dark tail tipped with gray.

male

female

Blue Grouse: *adults*

The Blue Grouse's confidence in its camouflage is so complete that it allows humans and other potential predators to approach far closer than appears prudent. This extreme adaptation has led to the common name of 'fool hen.' We have seen a Blue Grouse cross the road in front of a moving vehicle, jump up on the hood when the car screeched to a stop and proceed to pick insects off the windshield while the occupants stared in amazement, only inches away.

This bird's usual style is to remain hunkered on the ground hoping that its camouflage colors will protect it even as you walk right by. In emergencies its short, broad wings enable it to explode into flight, rising straight up in the air in a quick getaway and startling the intruder.

The male Blue Grouse advertises his presence from a perch in a conifer with a series of five to seven low hoots increasing in volume and tempo. His inflatable neck sacs amplify the sounds that lure in the females. The male and female engage in courtship dances; then the female wanders off on her own to lay her eggs.

Seasonal Occurrence & Local Range: *Year-round residents, Blue Grouse are widely distributed along the coast from B.C. through Washington and Oregon. During the breeding season they forage from sea level to the alpine. Unlike many birds that head down in elevation in winter, some Blue Grouse move up to subalpine forests, where they feed almost exclusively on conifer needles.*
Size: *about 51 cm (20 in.).*

WHITE-TAILED PTARMIGAN

Lagopus leucurus

This grouse is exclusively an alpine bird. In summer it is two-toned gray-brown above and white below, and can be told from all other ptarmigan by its white tail. Winter birds are all white. Up close, watch for the fully feathered 'snowshoe' feet.

White-tailed Ptarmigan: *breeding male*

It would be hard to imagine a better adapted alpine hiker than the White-tailed Ptarmigan. In summer the birds are a mottled lichen color, and in winter they turn snow white. Their feathered feet look like fluffy bedroom slippers but serve as snowshoes, keeping them aloft in soft snow. In severe weather they escape the worst by tunneling into the snow near willow bushes, where, safe from the howling winds, they nibble on willow buds.

White-tailed Ptarmigan nest in the alpine too, usually under a shrub but sometimes completely exposed. Even more so than their grouse relatives, they have come to rely completely on their cryptic coloration for protection since there are often no trees at all where they nest. A brooding female will remain sitting on her nest even if you walk right up to her. Nevertheless, this kind of situation is very stressful for her, and sensitive hikers can make a ptarmigan's tough life somewhat easier by staying some distance from a hen with eggs or chicks.

Seasonal Occurrence & Local Range: *White-tailed Ptarmigan are found year-round in alpine environments that are rich in dwarf willow.*
Size: *about 30 cm (12 in.).*

CALIFORNIA QUAIL
Callipepla californica

Quail are the smallest of our grouse-like birds. Typically they are seen bolting across roads or open spaces with their flapper-like head plumes bobbing furiously. The male has a black face with a bold white chin and brow stripe, a gray chest and a scaly belly. The female looks like a washed-out version of the male but with a smaller head plume.

California Quail: *male*

California Quail seem to be constantly on the move—scurrying from one place to another. This quail's call sounds like *chi-caa-go* with the accent on the middle syllable. Although they are nervous, skittery birds, quail will often investigate birders' attempts to sound like their brethren, so it's worth a try. It is difficult to find anyone who isn't amused by their appearance, although the more scientifically minded birdwatcher will be quick to remind him or herself that every aspect of these goofy-looking birds has a serious function.

Several California Quail families will band together into large coveys in winter and then disperse again in spring. When feeding, one quail will sit in a tree on guard for the others. Quail usually fly as an emergency measure—for a quick getaway. They typically hide in brush and scrub, and as these areas are 'cleaned up' or developed, quail populations disappear.

Quail young are extremely precocious. They are ready to run as soon as they emerge from the eggshell, and are flying within two weeks.

Seasonal Occurrence & Local Range: *California Quail are native to Oregon and introduced in Washington and B.C. They occur year-round in the lower elevation southern coastal areas of Vancouver Island and through Washington.* **Size:** *about 25 cm (10 in.).*

TURKEY VULTURE 🏔 🌲 🦅
Cathartes aura

Turkey Vultures are usually seen in flight with wings in a 'V' and wobbling rather drunkenly from side to side. Look for the two-toned wings: the wing lining is dark and the flight feathers are pale gray. The naked head is red in adults and gray in immatures but difficult to see at a distance.

Turkey Vulture: *in flight*

Turkey Vulture: *adult*

The Turkey Vultures' tilting flight is an energy-saving strategy. Without so much as turning their heads they can gain grand views of the country below as they search for meal opportunities. They also have a good sense of smell, which must be a blessing for finding the rotting carcasses on which they feed.

Vultures are seldom seen on land unless they have found a carcass or are perching in trees for the night. On land they are ungainly, but they are master riders of thermals—areas of warm, rising air. To cross the Strait of Juan de Fuca, Turkey Vultures need thermals, or they might find themselves stranded without the strength to flap their way to land. They spiral upwards within the thermal, then descend in a long glide to catch the next thermal going up.

In September you can watch hundreds of Turkey Vultures mustering for the big glide back to the Washington mainland. The southern tip of Vancouver Island and offshore islands such as Discovery and Chatham are good spots to watch from. Turkey Vultures use both the Gulf Islands and San Juans as stepping stones as they head south to California and Mexico where they spend the winter.

Seasonal Occurrence & Local Range: *This species is most abundant from April through September, from Vancouver Island south.*
Size: *about 69 cm (27 in.).*

NORTHERN HARRIER
Circus cyaneus

Long winged and long tailed, the Northern Harrier's most distinctive characteristics are its white rump and low gliding flight, plus the fact that it holds its wings up in a slight 'V.' The difference between the beautiful, pale gray males and the brownish females (who are larger) and immatures is striking. Note the males' black wing tips as well.

Northern Harrier: *female*

Northern Harriers are found in every kind of open country from the alpine to the airport. Usually you'll see them drifting low over fields, ready to pounce on some luckless meadow mouse. Their long, rudder-like tails enable them to maneuver sharply, as they quarter back and forth in search of prey.

The south coast around B.C.'s Boundary Bay and delta area of the Fraser Valley is a critical wintering area for these 'marsh hawks' as they were formerly known. More raptors can be seen in this region in winter than anywhere else in Canada, and over a third of these are harriers.

In winter Northern Harriers concentrate on voles and other small field and marsh mammals, their owl-like facial disks perhaps enabling them to focus sound and locate prey by their rustlings. In summer the birds opportunistically shift their attention to the hapless young ducks, coots and pheasants of the season, as well as the occasional frog or large insect.

Seasonal Occurrence & Local Range: *Northern Harriers migrate across southeastern Vancouver Island and the Fraser lowlands in March and April, and then again in September to November. They generally summer east of the Cascades and Coast Range, and in the Low Arctic.*
Size: *about 45 cm (18 in.).*

ACCIPITERS

NORTHERN GOSHAWK 🌲
Accipiter gentilis

COOPER'S HAWK 🌲 🌳
Accipiter cooperii

SHARP-SHINNED HAWK 🌲 🌳
Accipiter striatus

Accipiters' long tails and short, broad wings give them maneuverability at high speed, which they need as they pursue flying birds through trees and under bushes. Accipiters also have a flap-flap-flap-glide cadence to their wing beats. Goshawks are the largest and have a white line over the eye. Cooper's are larger than Sharp-shinneds and show a more rounded tail tip.

Northern Goshawk: *adult*

Northern Goshawks are often seen in mountainous terrain, patrolling forest edges or barreling through the woods after a hapless hare or grouse. As the first part of their name suggests, they breed north to Alaska and the Arctic. The second part of their name originally meant 'goose-hawk,' which overestimates their ferocity, but not by much. At the nest these are loud, aggressive birds that dive on all intruders, human and otherwise.

Separating Cooper's from Sharp-shinned Hawks is difficult. Even the sizes are problematic because a large female Sharp-shinned Hawk can approach the size of a male Cooper's. (Female birds of prey are always larger than their male counterparts.)

Cooper's are year-round urbanites, but Sharp-shinneds frequent cities only in winter. Both can be seen flap-flap-gliding though town, strafing starling and pigeon roosts, and hunting neighborhood bird feeders as systematically as if they were a trap line. The San Juan Islands and Victoria have the highest winter concentrations of Cooper's Hawks in North America.

You might mistake a passing Sharp-shinned for a similar-sized Merlin, but the Sharp-shinned relies on agility and branch dodging, whereas the Merlin relies on speed and attacks in the open air in typical falcon style.

Cooper's Hawk: *adult*

Sharp-shinned Hawk: *adult*

Seasonal Occurrence & Local Range: *Goshawks are uncommon residents along the coast. Cooper's are more southerly, not summering beyond northern Vancouver Island and wintering from southern B.C. to Costa Rica. 'Sharpies' are coastal migrants and winter visitors.*
Size: *Goshawk: about 52 cm (21 in.); Cooper's: about 42 cm (16 in.); Sharp-shinned: about 28 cm (11 in.).*

BUTEOS

RED-TAILED HAWK
Buteo jamaicensis

ROUGH-LEGGED HAWK
Buteo lagopus

Buteos are broad-winged, broad-tailed hawks with the perfect design for soaring aloft on thermals. 'Red-tails' usually have rusty red tails above, and their wings are pale underneath with a dark leading edge near the base. This description applies only to light morph adults; the dark or immature birds can be trickier to identify. The Rough-legged Hawk can be separated from the Red-tailed Hawk by its contrasting plumage—a wide, black band on a pale tail and dark underwing 'wrist marks.'

Red-tailed Hawk: *adult*

The Red-tailed Hawk is found virtually everywhere, from farmland to forest, sea level to timberline. Red-tails will eat almost any small animal, whereas Rough-legged Hawks are much more specialized—inclined to eat primarily small mammals. Red-tails are ever on the lookout for a free meal that has been captured by other raptors such as harriers. They have a piratical bent and are not above claiming another bird's kill.

The scream of a Red-tailed Hawk is commonly heard in movies and often misattributed to other larger birds of prey such as eagles because of its bloodcurdling qualities.

With experience, you will notice that the Red-tailed Hawk is heavier and more eagle-like than the Rough-legged and, conversely, that the Rough-legged is much more apt to 'wind hover,' holding its position in midair as it gazes downward at a potential meal.

Rough-legged Hawk: *adult*

Seasonal Occurrence & Local Range: *Red-tailed Hawks can be found year-round. Rough-legged Hawks occur on the coast only from October to March, and they may outnumber Red-tails in both species' favorite wintering grounds in the Fraser lowlands and Boundary Bay.*
Size: *both about 55 cm (22 in.).*

127

BALD EAGLE
Haliaeetus leucocephalus

GOLDEN EAGLE
Aquila chrysaetos

With its white head and tail, and brown body, a mature Bald Eagle is unmistakable. Immatures can be confused with Golden Eagles, but the latter always have golden feathers on the nape of their neck, and fully feathered legs. Young Bald Eagles have white-blotched wing linings, and older youngsters have blotchy bellies as well. Young Golden Eagles have white patches on the wings and tail.

Bald Eagle: *adult*

Bald Eagles are year-round feature birds of the West Coast. In spring they follow the herring runs and gather near Active Pass, Gabriola Island and the Queen Charlottes. In summer they search for surface-feeding fish, swooping and skimming the water to snatch their prey with fantastic aerial acrobatics. In fall and winter they congregate along rivers, where they feed on spawning salmon. The Squamish and Harrison rivers have become famous for winter eagle watching: on a good day thousands of eagles may be counted.

Bald Eagles nest in Puget Sound and the San Juans in greater numbers than anywhere else in the United States, but encroaching development is a problem for them. They require huge trees for nesting and prefer sites with a view, near water, as do humans. Belying their noble appearance, Bald Eagles have a high pitched, squeaky voice that sounds like a rusty clothes-line: *kleek-kik-ik-ik-ik*. Whereas Bald Eagles are fish eaters and scavengers, Golden Eagles are terrestrial birds that prey on small mammals, especially rabbits. For this reason, they are much less common near the coast and prefer drier, more open country further inland.

Seasonal Occurrence & Local Range: *Bald Eagles are widespread along the coast and are most concentrated in winter. Golden Eagles occur in hilly or mountainous country in the San Juans, the east coast of Vancouver Island and throughout the Fraser River lowlands.*
Size: *both about 90 cm (35 in.).*

OSPREY
Pandion haliaetus

Ospreys fly with a definite kink in the wrist, which makes them look 'M' shaped head-on. From below, Ospreys show a dark wrist patch. They have contrasting coloration, being mostly white underneath and dark above, with a dark line through the eye. Females have a faint necklace mark, and young birds have white-flecked rather than solid brown backs.

Osprey: *adult*

Ospreys or 'fish hawks' are truly cosmopolitan birds. Almost anywhere you travel around the world you can come across them patrolling high above lakes and peering into the water, although they are certainly more common in some places than in others.

It's a surprising sight to see a large hawk flying overhead suddenly tuck its wings and plummet into the water, throwing its feet forward at the last instant. Once soaked, the Osprey pushes down powerfully and rises in a great surge from the water to fly away, usually holding a fish in its talons. Its spiny feet are designed to grasp and hold onto slimy, slippery fish, and the birds carry their prey head forward to cut down on wind resistance.

Bald Eagles are not above pirating this prize if they can. The Osprey puts up a good fight though, screaming its indignation and twisting and turning in flight as it tries to lose its pursuer. On the other hand, an eagle that flies too close to an active Osprey nest will find itself under attack and the Osprey to be a formidable aggressor.

Seasonal Occurrence & Local Range: *Ospreys are most common in the lower third of B.C. and south of latitude 56°N. Most Ospreys depart in September and return in April, when open water assures their fish supply.* **Size:** *about 61 cm (24 in.).*

SMALL FALCONS

MERLIN
Falco columbarius

AMERICAN KESTREL
Falco sparverius

Falcons have swept-back, pointed wings, a long, narrow tail and rapid wing beats. These streamlined birds of prey are powerful dive-bombers. The Merlin is a dark, sleek falcon with a streaked breast. The American Kestrel is the flashiest, and the smallest, coastal falcon, with a strongly marked head, double sideburns and a cinnamon back and tail. Males have blue-gray wings. Both species are roughly jay sized. Kestrels have a buoyant flight style, and Merlins fly straight and fast.

Merlin: *female*

Merlins most often are seen hurtling at high speed into a flock of shorebirds or sweeping speedily above suburban neighborhoods in attempts to surprise House Sparrows. Formerly called the 'pigeon hawk,' they were renamed more elegantly to concur with the name used in Europe.

Although widely distributed throughout the area, Merlins are more likely to be seen in the winter when somewhat lighter-colored migrants come in from the north and the Interior. Although never plentiful, concentrations of Merlins occur in the Fraser lowlands.

American Kestrels are falcons of open country, and although they look to be only slightly smaller than Merlins, they weigh about half as much. They seek out perches such as power lines from which they scan fields and farmlands for mice or grasshoppers. Their fanned, rufous tail is a spectacular sight as they hover into position preparing to pounce on their prey. When agitated, which is often, they scream, *killy-killy-killy!* If you spend any time around them, it's a sound you'll soon get to know.

female

male

American Kestrel: *adults*

Seasonal Occurrence & Local Range: *Merlins breed all along the coast, and in winter, resident birds are joined by northern migrants. Kestrels are rare summer visitors on the B.C. coast and are uncommon in winter. They are more common further south in Washington and Oregon.*
Size: *Merlin: about 30 cm (12 in.); Kestrel: about 27 cm (10.5 in.).*

PEREGRINE FALCON
Falco peregrinus

GYRFALCON
Falco rusticolus

Peregrines are large, dark, slate-backed falcons that appear paler below. Their black helmet with Elvis-like sideburns can be seen at a distance. Gyrfalcons are larger, with less contrasting plumage.

Peregrine Falcon: *adult*

Whether they are nailing pigeons in urban concrete canyons or chasing seabirds above surging waves, Peregrines are the air-to-air missiles of the bird world. Sleek and powerful, these amazing birds dive in closed-winged stoops, which often culminate with the intended prey being violently knocked from the sky. Stoop speed is very difficult to measure, but experts agree it most likely exceeds 250 km/hr. (155 mi./hr.).

Coastal Peregrines tend to nest near colonies of nesting seabirds. In the Pacific Northwest the densest populations of both are found in the Queen Charlotte Islands. The seabirds provide the Peregrines with a summer source of food. Since they don't migrate very far, the West Coast population (Peale's subspecies of the Peregrine) was not affected by the pesticide DDT and is still flourishing, as are its now rapidly recovering inland relatives.

Gyrfalcons resemble a pale Peregrine on steroids. They can be fully twice the size of a Peregrine. Although faster and more powerful in flapping flight than a Peregrine, they rarely stoop with closed wings.

Seasonal Occurrence & Local Range: *Peregrines are widespread along the coast and inland. In winter they concentrate in southern coastal areas of B.C., but they are relatively rare in Washington and Oregon. Gyrfalcons winter here in very small numbers.*
Size: *Peregrine: about 46 cm (18 in.); Gyrfalcon: about 63 cm (25 in.).*

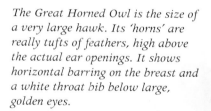

GREAT HORNED OWL
Bubo virginianus

The Great Horned Owl is the size of a very large hawk. Its 'horns' are really tufts of feathers, high above the actual ear openings. It shows horizontal barring on the breast and a white throat bib below large, golden eyes.

Great Horned Owl: *adult*

With its large size, low hooting call and ear tufts, the Great Horned Owl is the classic 'Halloween' owl. A formidable predator, the Great Horned has broad tastes—it will devour rats, rabbits, amphibians, cats, crows, other owls and even skunks. Its poorly developed sense of smell is an advantage in the last case, and discarded Great Horned Owl feathers are often identifiable by a simple sniff.

Deep, resonant hoots are often heard in January and February indicating that the Great Horned Owls are already nesting. They have no aversion to nesting in smelly clumps of parasitic 'witch's broom' mistletoe or in an abandoned (or commandeered) crow, hawk or even eagle nest. Great Horned Owls have been observed placidly brooding their eggs under a blanket of snow.

On late summer and autumn evenings, hunting parents may be seen accompanied by their fully grown young of the year. The raucous adolescents screech like a giant running shoe on a newly polished floor, which must make finding dinner even more difficult for the harried parents.

Seasonal Occurrence & Local Range: *Generally considered nonmigratory, Great Horned Owls are found almost any place where there are stands of large trees.*
Size: *about 56 cm (22 in.)*

PALE OWLS

SNOWY OWL
Nyctea scandiaca

BARN OWL
Tyto alba

Snowy Owls are large, white arctic owls with golden eyes and no ear tufts. The smaller Barn Owls are also pale but with a tawny back. Note the Barn Owl's heart-shaped facial disk, dark eyes and long legs. They look much more elongated than Snowy Owls and weigh 75 percent less.

Snowy Owl: *female*

Snowy Owls perch as motionless as soapstone carvings. Stoically confronting winter's worst, they watch and listen for the stirrings of voles. When the numbers of voles and arctic lemmings are low, many Snowy Owls head south to winter on the southern coast of B.C. through to Washington.

Some years, winter walkers can spot large numbers of Snowy Owls, but in other years they are rare. These 'ookpiks' choose log-covered beaches, barren islands and even airports for their southern sojourns; here they perch atop the highest vantage point they can find. When on the coast, they change their diet, preying heavily on small waterfowl such as Horned Grebes and Bufflehead.

Barn Owls are year-round residents who prefer agricultural lands and grasslands, although in some areas they will inhabit the edges of mixed woodlands. Depending on the number of voles, they may breed year-round. Their numbers are precarious because of the loss of agricultural lands and proper nest sites such as, of course, barns. However, they will use nest boxes and have responded well to help with accommodations.

Barn Owl: *adult*

Seasonal Occurrence & Local Range: *Snowy Owls visit from November through March, most numerously at Boundary Bay, Roberts Banks and along the farmlands and dunes of northwest Washington. Although Barn Owls are almost cosmopolitan, southern Vancouver Island and the Fraser farmlands lie at the northern edge of their range.*
Size: *Snowy: about 58 cm (23 in.); Barn: about 41 cm (16 in.).*

135

LARGE, DARK-EYED OWLS 🌲

BARRED OWL
Strix varia

SPOTTED OWL
Strix occidentalis

Barred Owls are fairly large, gray-brown owls with a round head and a vertically striped belly. Spotted Owls are similar but slightly smaller and more chocolate brown in color; their underparts and back show creamy-white, horizontal blotches or 'spots.' Barred Owls are famous for their loud distinctive call, who...who cooks...you-all; Spotteds call who cooks...you.

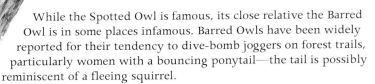

Barred Owl: *adult*

While the Spotted Owl is famous, its close relative the Barred Owl is in some places infamous. Barred Owls have been widely reported for their tendency to dive-bomb joggers on forest trails, particularly women with a bouncing ponytail—the tail is possibly reminiscent of a fleeing squirrel.

Spotted Owls need large expanses of old growth forest, whereas Barred Owls can also make do in second growth forests; both use large hollow trees for nesting.

Barred Owls have greatly expanded their range in recent decades. This expansion may be a problem for the less adaptable Spotted Owl, for the two species' ranges now overlap. In these areas of overlap the two owls compete and even interbreed with one another.

Why is the Spotted Owl having such a hard time surviving when, in contrast, the Barred Owl is expanding its range? These sorts of questions are much easier to ask than to answer, but it seems that habitat changes and resulting shifts in the distribution and abundance of predators, prey, competitors and possibly even parasites or diseases figure prominently. To make things even more difficult, the exact numbers and locations of both species have always been difficult to determine because the birds are secretive, camouflaged and active only at night.

Spotted Owl: *adult*

Seasonal Occurrence & Local Range: *Barred Owls, originally denizens of the dark, swampy forests of the southeastern U.S., are expanding their range into the West Coast region. The Spotted Owl is found from B.C. to Mexico where old growth forests still stand.*
Size: *Barred: about 53 cm (21 in.); Spotted: about 43 cm (17 in.).*

SMALL OWLS

NORTHERN
SAW-WHET OWL
Aegolius acadicus

WESTERN SCREECH-OWL
Otus kennicottii

NORTHERN PYGMY-OWL
Glaucidium gnoma

The Northern Saw-whet Owl lacks ear tufts and has a stubby appearance because of its short tail. Its yellow eyes and pronounced facial disk without black borders are striking. The immature Saw-whet is rusty colored with a white triangle between its eyes. The Western Screech-Owl is small and brown, with ear tufts. The smallest of the coastal owls, the Northern Pygmy-Owl has no ear tufts, two black 'eye-spots' on the back of its neck and a long tail that it tends to flick.

Northern Saw-whet Owl: *adult*

During bad weather Northern Saw-whet Owls will roost without moving for days at a time, and they are also extremely tame. As a result, some of them have been collected accidentally by tree cutters at Christmas, to later emerge from the wrapped trees inside people's homes. Although named for the sound of a saw being sharpened, their more common call is a long series of *too-too-too-too*'s given two or three times a second. Northern Saw-whets specialize in eating deer mice, and in especially good mouse years, males may be able to provide food for more than one nesting partner.

The Western Screech-Owl is especially vocal at the beginning of its nesting season in February and March. Its call is a series of identical notes that start slowly and gradually speed up (like a ball bouncing lower and lower to an eventual stop). This owl prefers suburbia or the borders of woodlands, where it is often seen at dusk and dawn.

Northern Pygmy-Owls hunt by day and are frequently seen during the day, perched atop a snag, looking for all the world like a ball of moss or last summer's fruit. If you try to imitate their call (whistle while attempting to say *kook* about once every two seconds), you may attract the owls, or small birds intent on driving owls away. These irate songbirds can show up in numbers, intending to mob this feisty, little predator. The two spots on the back of its head are fake eyes, helpful in intimidating such attacking birds.

Western Screech-Owl: *adult*

Northern Pygmy-Owl: *red phase*

Seasonal Occurrence & Local Range: *All three species are widespread but more common from southern B.C. south. Western Screech-Owls are low elevation residents; the other two species migrate upslope in summer and back down in winter. Northern Saw-whets range up to the Queen Charlottes, where there is an endemic subspecies.*
Size: *Saw-whet and Screech: about 20 cm (8 in.); Pygmy: about 18 cm (7 in.).*

SHORT-EARED OWL
Asio flammeus

Look at sunrise or sunset for a tawny, long-winged, blunt-headed bird flying with erratic wing beats. Underneath the wings, dark wrist marks are visible. Its pale belly shows vertical stripes. Forget the short ears; they are almost never visible.

Short-eared Owl: *adult*

Looking almost headless, Short-eared Owls flap with lazy, irregular wing beats across open areas, often in broad daylight. When they land on a post and gaze at you, however, there's no mistaking the Short-eared's owlish face with its flat facial disks and striking yellow eyes.

Short-eared Owls occur from sea level to the timberline—wherever there are grassy fields and meadows. Airports and farmlands are equally suitable venues for this owl, as it beats over grassy areas searching for voles. Because Short-eared Owls lay their eggs on the ground in grassy fields, their nests are often destroyed by farm machinery. Although they used to be abundant in the Fraser River area and on Vancouver Island, they have declined there and across the continent in recent years.

Short-eared Owls and Northern Harriers use very similar habitats and prey items, and it is interesting to note that the harrier is the most owl-like of all the hawks.

Seasonal Occurrence & Local Range: *Short-eared Owls are cosmopolitan birds. They are more common in winter in southern British Columbia than Washington and Oregon; the Fraser River delta is the main wintering area in B.C.*
Size: *about 38 cm (15 in.).*

 **BELTED KINGFISHER**

Ceryle alcyon

Belted Kingfishers are medium-sized birds with blue and white markings, rapid flight and a loud rattling call. They appear to have over-sized heads relative to their body; a ragged, blue crest and thick, dagger-like bill add to this impression. Males have a blue-gray breast band; females have an additional sporty, red vest.

female

male

Belted Kingfisher: *adults*

Wherever there is good fishing on either salt or fresh water, you can expect to find Belted Kingfishers. Perched on an overhanging branch, they gaze into the water searching for fish, then plunge in headfirst after their prey, often after hovering in midair.

Kingfishers are feisty loners who constantly seem to be in a state of agitation, judging by their loud, rattling calls and their frequent habit of chasing other kingfishers away from their waterfront property. Only at mating time do they tolerate one another, and they rarely let people get very close.

In spring the kingfishers pair up and set about excavating a burrow in a sand or clay bank in which to raise their family. They use their beaks to dig, pushing out the dirt with their weak feet. The female broods while the male does double duty fishing—feeding both his mate and the youngsters until the young are feathered. To teach their young to plunge after food, kingfishers drop dead fish into the water. As soon as their offspring are proficient fishers, the parents once again go their separate ways.

Seasonal Occurrence & Local Range: *Of the many species of kingfisher worldwide, the Belted Kingfisher is the only one in the Pacific Northwest. If their inland haunts freeze, kingfishers will bullet to the coast or the nearest open water.*
Size: *about 33 cm (13 in.).*

DOVES

ROCK DOVE
Columba livia

BAND-TAILED PIGEON
Columba fasciata

MOURNING DOVE
Zenaida macroura

Rock Doves or 'domestic pigeons' come in a variety of colors—black, gray, brown or white, and combinations thereof. Typically they are gray with a white rump and a dark tail band. Larger Band-tailed Pigeons have a white collar on their nape, a yellow bill and legs, and a broad, pale band on the tail. Mourning Doves are small, slim doves with a long, white-edged, pointed tail.

Rock Dove: *adult*

Rock Doves are the wild or 'feral' version of the domestic pigeon. Other than in name, there is no distinction between pigeons and doves. Introduced from Europe, Rock Doves have settled in wherever there are cities, towns, farms or grain elevators.

Clapping their wings in rapid flight, they can give even a Peregrine Falcon a run for its money, and beginning birders sometimes mistake Rock Doves for falcons, just to make things more confusing.

Doves share their parental duties, the female incubating by day and the male taking on the night shift. The parents must drink plenty of water with their seed grain diet to produce 'pigeon milk' in their crops, a mucous-like mixture of fluids that they feed to their young. Rock Doves may raise as many as four broods in a year, even though they only have one or two young at a time.

In fall flocks of handsome Band-tailed Pigeons descend to gobble the fruits of arbutus, mountain ash and oak trees. In spring they congregate around gravel pits and intertidal flats because they need calcium to make eggs and to help them with their 'milk' production. They usually nest in big Douglas-firs in flimsy platforms of loose sticks that, with luck, will last long enough to raise their single young.

Mourning Doves occur in low numbers in southern coastal B.C. and Washington. Historically they were more common in coastal Washington than they are today.

Band-tailed Pigeon: *adult*

Mourning Dove: *adult*

Seasonal Occurrence & Local Range: *Rock Doves are abundant year-round in metropolitan areas. Band-tailed Pigeons are most common from spring through fall. Mourning Doves are uncommon throughout our area year-round.* **Size:** *Rock and Mourning Doves: about 30 cm (12 in.); Band-tailed Pigeon: about 38 cm (15 in.).*

COMMON NIGHTHAWK
Chordeiles minor

Nighthawks are nightjars, not hawks, and as such they have neither a hooked bill nor strong talons. A white throat, long tail and long, pointed wings with bold, white wing bars across them are the field marks of the Common Nighthawk.

Common Nighthawk: *adult*

The sound of Common Nighthawks is the sound of summer evenings. A single, nasal *bjeet!* call, repeated frequently, is your clue to look skyward for nighthawks. These birds have an erratic, bat-like flight, which is not surprising since both bats and nightjars scoop insects from the air for a living. Nighthawks have a huge mouth outlined with stiff bristles to catch those morsels that weren't perfectly lined up with the gape.

During the day, the nighthawks roost by lying lengthwise along a branch or hunkering down on a flat, gravel roof. Although strong fliers, they are weak footed and seldom walk. So perfect is their camouflage that, at rest, they are almost impossible to see, even when you are staring right at them. They lay their eggs directly on the ground.

As a territorial display, male Common Nighthawks climb high in the sky and then swoop down, pulling out of the dive and spreading the wing feathers at the last second to produce a wonderful sound, like the strumming of a giant rubber band.

Seasonal Occurrence & Local Range: *Common Nighthawks are found throughout the area from late May through early September, including most towns and cities. They winter in South America as far south as Argentina.* **Size:** *about 23 cm (9 in.).*

RUFOUS HUMMINGBIRD
Selasphorus rufus

Hummingbirds are tiny, fast flying and iridescent. A long, stiletto bill, and a helicopter-like ability to fly in any direction or hover on the spot, assist them in their nectar-sipping lifestyle. The Rufous male is almost entirely orange above, with a glistening, orange-red throat patch. The Rufous female is green above and white below, with rufous sides and small spots on the throat.

male

female

Rufous Hummingbird: *adults*

Rufous Hummingbirds are the common hummingbird of the West Coast. In early spring they leave their wintering grounds in Mexico and stitch their way north, flower to flower, following the early sea level bloom of red-flowering currants and salmonberry. The feisty males arrive in March, followed a few weeks later by the females.

Hummingbirds have to be 'power smart' because they are raging, metabolic furnaces. The males defend feeding territories pugnaciously, driving all other hummers away from the feeder or patch of flowers that serves as their insurance policy for their high energy needs.

The females are devoted single parents. They build their nest on top of cedar boughs, weaving together lichens and down with spider webs. In the breeding season watch for them picking insects out of flowers and spider webs to increase the protein intake for their growing young.

In Haida legends hummingbirds brought joy and healing. They still do today.

Seasonal Occurrence & Local Range: *Rufous Hummingbirds are found all along the coast. Arriving in early March, the males depart as early as June or July and harvest nectar from late blooming, high elevation flowers on their return journey south. The females and young depart in late August and September.*
Size: *about 9 cm (3.5 in.).*

ANNA'S HUMMINGBIRD
Calypte anna

CALLIOPE HUMMINGBIRD
Stellula calliope

Anna's Hummingbird is the same size as the Rufous, but males have a metallic, rose-red crown as well as throat. Females are green above, show no rufous on the sides or tail and have a speckling of red on the throat. Calliope Hummingbirds are smaller and have a shorter bill. Notice the purple throat patch on the Calliope males—a streakier pattern than in other hummingbirds.

female

male

Anna's Hummingbird: *adults*

Anna's are the least migratory of our hummingbirds. They spread north from California about 30 years ago, following hummingbird feeders up the coast. Anna's tend to set up camp in gardens that bloom year-round or where they can rely on a hummingbird feeder to be maintained over winter. They nest in late winter and early spring, usually in February and March. An adventurous Anna's once showed up in Hazelton in northern British Columbia and was sent south to a University of British Columbia hummingbird researcher to be cared for over the winter.

Calliopes are the smallest birds in North America and their scientific name translates as 'beautiful little star.' With their white-streaked gorget that seems too big for the bird that carries it, they look as cute as can be, an appearance that belies their feisty and quarrelsome temperament (a trait common to all hummingbirds).

Seasonal Occurrence & Local Range: *Anna's are seen locally in Washington, Oregon and southern B.C., where year-round gardens and feeders sustain them. Tiny Calliope Hummingbirds are summer residents of mountain meadows. They occasionally pass through coastal Washington and B.C. on their way to the Interior.*
Size: *Anna's: about 9 cm (3.5 in.); Calliope about 7 cm (2.75 in.).*

SWIFTS

BLACK SWIFT
Cypseloides niger

VAUX'S SWIFT
Chaetura vauxi

Swifts whirl and dive on boomerang-shaped wings. Their flight pattern is a combination of rapid, 'twinkling' wing beats and stiff-winged glides. Black Swifts are uniformly dark with a slightly forked tail. Vaux's Swifts are smaller and browner, showing pale gray on the throat. You could mistake Vaux's for swallows, but they appear more cigar shaped, and the elbows of their long wings bend closer to the body.

Vaux's Swift: *adult*

Swifts belong to a family called Apodidae, meaning that they have very little in the way of feet ('pod' means 'feet,' so 'a-pod' means 'no feet'). These tiny feet are a consequence of the birds' aerial lifestyle. Swifts feed and copulate in flight, alighting only to raise their young. They use their tiny feet merely for clinging to the surfaces where they nest, which may be cliff faces (for Black Swifts) or hollow trees (for Vaux's). Despite their resemblance to swallows, swifts are more closely related to hummingbirds.

Foraging far from their breeding sites, swifts ride on storm fronts and sail on approaching weather systems, harvesting flying insects for their young. The young are able to drop their body temperature and go into an energy-saving state of torpor for long periods, a useful adaptation when the parents are off feeding and the nest is shrouded in cool mist.

Seasonal Occurrence & Local Range: *Swifts visit the West Coast from May through September. Black Swifts range to northern B.C.; Vaux's breed north to southern Alaska, although they are far more common in the south.* **Size**: *Black Swift: about 18 cm (7 in.); Vaux's Swift: about 11 cm (4.5 in.).*

147

BARN SWALLOW
Hirundo rustica

Swallows are blunt-headed, short-necked birds with long, pointed wings. They have more of a tail than do swifts, and their wings are broader and less swept back. Barn Swallows are blue-black above and orangy-rust below, with a deeply forked tail.

Barn swallow: *adult*

In spring and summer there are five species of swallow that are commonly seen in coastal areas, and of all, Barn Swallows are the most common. Barn Swallows are appreciated for both their beauty and their practicality. They are natural pest controllers, feeding on flying insects, and their fork-tailed acrobatics are a delight to behold.

When not swooping after insects, they perch conspicuously on wires, often in mixed feeding flocks, since swallows tend to assemble in areas where insects are hatching, swarming or courting.

Barn Swallows build their mud nests on any structure that offers overhead protection from the elements. They may become highly accepting of human presence yet will fearlessly dive-bomb intruders such as crows or snakes that pose a threat to their young. Unfortunately, not everyone appreciates the craftsmanship of their mud nests, and many a Barn Swallow family has been unceremoniously scraped off a building just as the nesting season has begun.

This species is also found in Europe, where it is simply referred to as 'the swallow.'

Seasonal Occurrence & Local Range: *Barn Swallows breed on the West Coast and are seen from March through September. They winter from the southern United States to Central and South America.*
Size: about 17 cm (6.75 in.)—much of it tail.

CLIFF SWALLOW
Hirundo pyrrhonota

Cliff Swallows have a color scheme similar to Barn Swallows but with a square-tipped tail, buffy rump and a buffy patch on the forehead.

Cliff Swallow: *adult*

Clouds of Cliff Swallows are often seen swooping around bridges or near cliff walls above water, where they construct colonies of gourd-shaped nests. Master mud masons, Cliff Swallows roll mud into balls with their bills, then press the pellets together. After several days of solid work, the nest is complete. The parents brood their eggs and peer out the circular neck of their nest with their gleaming eyes, watching the world go by. This is a useful pastime because they can see from which directions come the birds returning with food—an advantage of colonial living.

Cliff Swallows have been found to take advantage of their neighbors in another more insidious way. They have been observed sneaking into a neighbor's home to lay an egg, much like female American Coots will often do. And, strange as it seems, they have also been seen flying into a nest carrying an egg in their beak. The basic principle here is that you can raise more young if you enlist the help of other females, but the question of how this can work when all the females are doing it to one another is currently being debated by ornithologists.

Seasonal Occurrence & Local Range: *Cliff Swallows are breeders throughout our area and are seen from March through September.*
Size: *about 14 cm (5.5 in.).*

149

OTHER SWALLOWS

TREE SWALLOW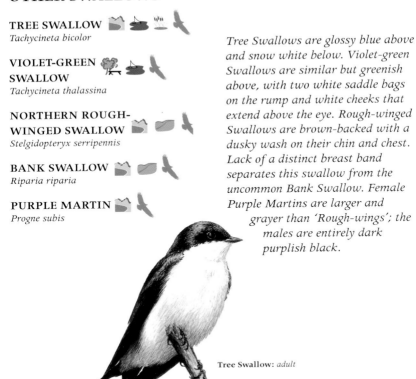
Tachycineta bicolor

VIOLET-GREEN SWALLOW
Tachycineta thalassina

NORTHERN ROUGH-WINGED SWALLOW
Stelgidopteryx serripennis

BANK SWALLOW
Riparia riparia

PURPLE MARTIN
Progne subis

Tree Swallows are glossy blue above and snow white below. Violet-green Swallows are similar but greenish above, with two white saddle bags on the rump and white cheeks that extend above the eye. Rough-winged Swallows are brown-backed with a dusky wash on their chin and chest. Lack of a distinct breast band separates this swallow from the uncommon Bank Swallow. Female Purple Martins are larger and grayer than 'Rough-wings'; the males are entirely dark purplish black.

Tree Swallow: *adult*

Tree Swallows are early scouts of spring, often arriving before the first hatches of insects. They are more flexible than other swallows, making do with seeds and berries while they wait for spring warmth to arrive and awaken overwintering bugs. These swallows nest naturally in standing snags, usually near water. They must compete with starlings, bluebirds, House Wrens and House Sparrows for these cavity nest sites, which sadly are becoming increasingly rare because of forestry and urban development.

Violet-green Swallow: *adult*

Enterprising Violet-green Swallows also jump the gun on spring, arriving in late February from Central America and Mexico. They are loosely colonial where rock faces provide ample nesting cavities, and they will readily adapt to nest boxes. They can be seen hawking mosquitoes and other insects over towns or forests during summer.

Rough-winged Swallows are the color of the sandy banks where they live. These loners nest in burrows along riverbanks, enjoying their own private piece of waterfront. However, they don't mind joining a crowd to feast on insect hatches over rivers or wetlands. When they pause to rest on wires with other swallows, Rough-winged swallows are clay-colored beads in an otherwise brightly colored string.

Rare and local, Purple Martins summer in southern B.C. and Washington near estuarine mud flats where nest boxes provide starling-free accommodations.

Northern Rough-winged Swallow: *adult*

Seasonal Occurrence & Local Range: *These swallows winter in South America and are seen here in the summer. Tree Swallows arrive in early March and depart in August. Violet-greens arrive in late February; Rough-winged Swallows are here from April through August; and Bank Swallows are occasional migrants. Purple Martins are uncommon and local breeders.* **Size:** *all about 14 cm (5.5 in.), except the Purple Martin: 20 cm (8 in.).*

SMALL WOODPECKERS

HAIRY WOODPECKER
Picoides villosus

DOWNY WOODPECKER
Picoides pubescens

THREE-TOED WOODPECKER
Picoides tridactylus

Woodpeckers have a swooping, zig-zag flight. They cling vertically to trees using their stiff tail feathers as a prop and their unusual feet (two toes point forward, two toes backward) to anchor them. Hairy and Downy Woodpeckers are black and white with a white back. To sort them out, notice overall size and proportions of the head. The smaller Downy also has a proportionately smaller bill (remember DD for 'Diminutive Downy' and HH for 'Huge Hairy'). Males of both species have red on the back of their head. Three-toed Woodpeckers are about the size of a Hairy but have barred sides and back, and a yellow crown on the males.

Hairy Woodpecker: *male*

Downy Woodpeckers have adapted well to small patches of mixed deciduous forest and urban woodlots, whereas the larger Hairy Woodpecker prefers coniferous forests and is a warier bird by nature. A pair of Hairy Woodpeckers may stay loosely associated within a territory all year round and, indeed, for their entire lives. The pair will regularly visit a suet feeder, but sometimes the female has to slip in quick visits around her domineering mate's feeding schedule.

If you are hiking in the mountains, especially in freshly burned areas, you might encounter a Three-toed Woodpecker, a bird of higher elevation forests. Unlike its deep-drilling relatives, the Three-toed Woodpecker finds its food by flicking bark off trees with glancing blows of the bill. True to its name, it also has three toes instead of the usual four of other woodpeckers.

Woodpeckers excavate their own nest sites, most often in dead or near dying trees. The nest is lined with the wood chips from their chiseling. Typically, female woodpeckers incubate the eggs during the day, and the males have the night. A new nest is usually excavated every year, which provides essential real estate for other cavity nesters such as owls, chickadees, nuthatches and even ducks.

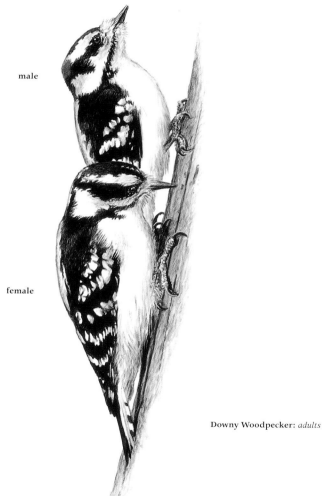

male

female

Downy Woodpecker: *adults*

Seasonal Occurrence & Local Range: *All are residents throughout the West Coast region, although Downy Woodpeckers are the most abundant species near settled areas.*
Size: *Hairy: about 24 cm (9.5 in.); Downy: about 17 cm (6.5 in.); Three-toed: about 22 cm (8.5 in.).*

RED-BREASTED SAPSUCKER 🌲
Sphyrapicus ruber

The Red-breasted Sapsucker is a stunning, noisy woodpecker with a solid red head and breast, and a black and white body. It resembles the Red-headed Woodpecker of the east and is often mistakenly called by that name. The sexes look alike.

Red-breasted Sapsucker: *adult*

Sapsuckers have adopted a variation on the woodpecker theme. They drill tidy, parallel lines of 'wells' in the bark of trees. The wells fill with sap, which attracts insects, giving the sapsucker the choice between sweet sap or tasty bugs. Sapsuckers don't actually suck sap—they lap it up with a fringed tongue tip that resembles a paintbrush.

Hummingbirds often associate with sapsuckers and sip sap at their wells too. This source of nutrition is so important that hummingbirds will defend feeding territories around active sapsucker wells.

Although shyer than most woodpeckers, the Red-breasted Sapsucker is common, especially in mid-elevation hemlock forests, and it is especially abundant in the Queen Charlotte Islands.

It has two close relatives—the Yellow-bellied in northern B.C. and east of the Rockies, and the Red-naped Sapsucker in the interior valleys of southern B.C., Washington and Oregon. Red-breasted and Red-naped Sapsuckers occasionally hybridize along the crest of the Cascade and Coast ranges. At one time all three were considered a single species, and since history is prone to repeating itself, they might become one species again.

Seasonal Occurrence & Local Range: *Red-breasted Sapsuckers are found in mid- and south coastal British Columbia, south to California. Interior populations migrate to coastal forests in winter, but coastal birds usually stay at mid-elevations. In periods of very cold weather, when the sap stops flowing in the trees, these birds move downhill to valley bottom woodlands and gardens.*
Size: *about 20 cm (8 in.).*

NORTHERN FLICKER

Colaptes auratus

This unusual looking woodpecker has bright, salmon-colored wing and tail linings, a dapper suit of fine, black stripes on a brown background, a spotted breast and a black bib. A flash of white on the rump as the bird flies off in an undulating flight is unmistakable. Males are distinguished by a red mustache.

male

female

Northern Flicker: *adults*

Northern Flickers are the most common suburban and rural woodpecker on the coast and a bit of an oddball in the woodpecker family. They spend a great deal of time on the ground eating ants, so it is not uncommon to startle yourself and a flicker when you are walking in the woods. These flickers can extend their tongue a good five centimeters (two inches) beyond the tip of their long, curved beak. When retracted, the tongue slips into a double sheath that wraps around the back of the skull, just beneath the skin. The tip of the tongue is barbed and coated with sticky saliva to capture and hold wriggling insects.

Northern Flickers let their presence be known by sending out a piercing single *pee-yew!* Their call is a softer version of the Pileated's and sounds like their name: *flicka-flicka-flicka.* In the absence of dead, hollow trees, flickers will also seek out metal stove pipes and other reverberating objects on which to drum loudly to attract mates and claim territories.

In winter Northern Flickers switch to a diet of berries and fruit but can benefit greatly from backyard suet feeders, especially when snow is on the ground.

Seasonal Occurrence & Local Range: *Northern Flickers are widespread throughout the Pacific Northwest Coast area. They can be seen year-round but are rare in northern B.C. in winter.*
Size: *about 30 cm (12 in.).*

LEWIS' WOODPECKER 🌲

Melanerpes lewis

The Lewis' is a greenish black woodpecker with a pink belly, gray breast speckled with black, gray collar and a red face. This woodpecker appears very dark at a distance, and young birds are much more brownish gray than the adults.

Lewis' Woodpecker: *adult*

Lewis' Woodpecker is an oddball, and it is also very rare on the coast. If it were more like any of its relatives, we would simply mention it in passing, but since it is so unmistakable, it deserves special treatment. Among other peculiarities, the Lewis' is the only woodpecker that doesn't mind perching on power lines and other sorts of wires, and it also gets much of its food by catching insects in midair, as well as eating berries and nuts.

For a while, ornithologists placed Lewis' Woodpecker in its own genus, but it is now considered one of the *Melanerpes*—a diverse group of woodpeckers that includes the well-known Red-headed Woodpecker of the east. Once you start talking to people about birds, you'll find that any woodpecker with red on it sometimes gets called the 'Red-headed Woodpecker,' but the true 'Redheads' don't live anywhere near the West Coast.

Lewis' Woodpeckers used to breed along the coast in standing dead snags in burned over areas and open forests. However, the removal of such trees, which were essential for nesting, as well as the decline in numbers of Garry oak, have caused the species to decline dramatically in our area. At present, Lewis' is more common in Washington than it is in British Columbia.

Seasonal Occurrence & Range: *Lewis' Woodpecker is a rare visitor along the coast north to the Fraser delta and Vancouver Island. It is seen throughout the year but mostly in summer.*
Size: *about 27 cm (10.5 in.).*

PILEATED WOODPECKER

Dryocopus pileatus

The crow-sized Pileated Woodpecker is the largest woodpecker of the coast. Male Pileated Woodpeckers can be distinguished by their red mustache and a red crest that extends down the forehead; the red in the female is strictly in her topknot. This species' underwings flash white in flight.

Pileated Woodpecker: *male*

Pileateds are the woodpecker kings and queens of mature coastal forests.

Pileated means 'capped' and refers to the magnificent, red crest. The sight of these big birds swooping through the woods is a thrill indeed, and their wild and maniacal *wucka wucka wucka* call can stop you in your tracks.

The first clue that you are in Pileated territory is often the sight of large, door-shaped holes in trees. Pileateds chisel elongate holes because their long neck gives them the reach that short-necked woodpeckers lack. Since all that chiseling can wear a woodpecker's bill down, the bill continues to grow throughout the bird's life.

Pileated Woodpecker pairs usually require a fairly large territory—a square kilometer or more where they are year-round residents. This requirement, combined with their need for old growth forests, means that these birds are never abundant.

Seasonal Occurrence & Local Range: *This species is seen year-round in mature forests of southern British Columbia, Washington and Oregon.*
Size*: about 41 cm (16 in.).*

KINGBIRDS

EASTERN KINGBIRD
Tyrannus tyrannus

WESTERN KINGBIRD
Tyrannus verticalis

Kingbirds are large flycatchers, and most are boldly marked. Eastern Kingbirds are dark gray with a white underside and tail tip. Western Kingbirds have a gray head, dark wings, a white-edged, dark tail and a yellow belly.

Eastern Kingbird: *adult*

Kingbirds are not really coastal birds, but because they are bigger and flashier than our other flycatchers, they catch the attention of birdwatchers when they appear. Both the Eastern and Western Kingbird are more common in the Interior, and the Eastern is the more abundant of the two along the B.C. and Washington coast. The Western is found more commonly along the coasts of Oregon and California.

Kingbirds get their name from the belligerent way they defend their nesting territory. The Eastern is especially vocal, and its harsh, scolding *kitter-kitter* calls have sent many a crow, hawk or house cat hurrying for cover. When enraged, which is often, both sorts of kingbirds can raise a small patch of red-orange feathers on the crown of the head; this patch remains hidden at other times.

Keen birdwatchers will double check all Western Kingbird sightings, especially in the fall, on the off chance that they are looking at a rare, vagrant Tropical Kingbird. This species has a somewhat forked tail with no white edging.

Western Kingbird: *adult*

Seasonal Occurrence & Local Range: *Both kingbird species are uncommon summer visitors or migrants, although the Eastern occasionally breeds here. They are seen in relatively open country along the coast and on the islands.* **Size:** *both about 20 cm (8 in.).*

🌲 ⛰ LARGE FLYCATCHERS

OLIVE-SIDED FLYCATCHER
Contopus borealis

WESTERN WOOD-PEWEE
Contopus sordidulus

Flycatchers sit on an exposed perch and dart out after insects, usually returning to the spot from which they started. Olive-sided Flycatchers wear an olive 'vest coat,' with white tufts flanking their lower back. They are proportionately short tailed. Western Wood-Pewee are dark, brownish-gray birds with double wing bars and a slightly crested head.

Olive-sided Flycatcher: *adult*

Some groups within the flycatcher family are almost impossible to distinguish with certainty, so some birders are happy to call them flycatchers and leave it at that. Nevertheless, for those who thrive on puzzles, flycatcher calls and habitat are good clues to unraveling the difficulties of these birds' identification.

The Olive-sided Flycatcher's belly-up-to-the-bar call makes it a favorite with many birders. *Quick-three-beers!,* it cries—loudly and clearly. In late summer it changes its tune to an enthusiastic *pip-pip-pip!* It's a good thing this feisty, little bird has such a distinctive call because it is often difficult to spot. Look for a big-headed silhouette perched on the tip of a topmost, dead limb of a mature conifer.

A Western Wood-Pewee perches on the edge of a forest clearing near the top of a tree, quiet until it spots a wasp or fly. Then it sallies forth to snap up its victim. A burry, descending *peeer* is the hallmark of this bird. Pewees aren't as small as the *Empidonax* flycatchers, but they are named for their call, not their size.

Western Wood-Pewee: *adult*

Seasonal Occurrence & Local Range: *Olive-sided Flycatchers are widespread along the coast from March to September, especially at higher elevations. Western Wood-Pewees are also widespread, from March to September.* **Size**: *Olive-sided: about 18 cm (7 in.); Pewee: about 15 cm (6 in.).*

EMPIDONAX FLYCATCHERS

PACIFIC-SLOPE FLYCATCHER 🌲
Empidonax difficilis

HAMMOND'S FLYCATCHER 🌲 ⛰
Empidonax hammondii

WILLOW FLYCATCHER 🌳 🌲
Empidonax traillii

ALDER FLYCATCHER 🌳
Empidonax alnorum

Empidonax *flycatchers are a group of small, very similar birds with wing bars and, typically, eye-rings. Pacific-slope Flycatchers have a slightly tufted head, an almond shaped eye-ring and a yellowish wash underneath. Hammond's are dull olive in color, with two pale wing bars and a conspicuous eye-ring. They habitually flick their wings and tail. Willows and Alders have double wing bars and lack a conspicuous eye-ring. Often the songs of* Empidonax *are their most distinctive feature.*

Pacific-slope Flycatcher: *adult*

When it comes to identification, the Latin epithet *difficilis* says it all, yet the Pacific-slope Flycatcher's almond-shaped eye-ring and incessant *su-wheet* call are good clues to sorting out this common West Coast flycatcher. Formerly the Western Flycatcher, this species was split into the Pacific-slope Flycatcher and Cordilleran Flycatcher in 1989. The Pacific-slope Flycatcher prefers moist woods and coniferous forests with deciduous understory. Ladybugs are a favorite food within its insect diet, despite the fact that these beetles are distasteful to most birds.

Hammond's Flycatchers move north in late April with the early spring vanguard of Ruby-crowned Kinglets. There is little to distinguish Hammond's Flycatchers on looks alone, and even then they are usually invisible in the upper canopy, only occasionally dropping down to be observed. Hammond's are best distinguished by their sharp *pick!* call note and by habitat. Enjoying the high life, these birds forage for insects from the top branches of big evergreens, often at high elevations.

The Willow Flycatcher is virtually indistinguishable from the Alder Flycatcher until it opens its beak. A sneezy *fitz-bew* is the insistent call of the Willow Flycatcher. The Alder Flycatcher has an accented *fee-BEE-o*. Of all the flycatchers, the Willow Flycatcher is the last to show up from Central America, usually arriving in late May. It haunts brushy environments and is not adverse to urban areas where shrubby thickets provide adequate food and cover, but in recent years its numbers have diminished owing to habitat loss.

Hammond's Flycatcher: *breeding*

Willow Flycatcher: *adult*

Seasonal Occurrence & Local Range: *Pacific-slope and Hammond's Flycatchers are common below 1200 meters (about 4000 feet) from late April to September. Willow Flycatchers are found from the north end of Vancouver Island south through Washington and Oregon during the breeding season. Alder Flycatchers range from central B.C. north through Alaska.*
Size*: all species about 14 cm (5.5 in.).*

LARKS

HORNED LARK
Eremophila alpestris

SKY LARK
Alauda arvensis

Larks are ground-dwelling birds that walk rather than hop, and fly high in their courtship displays. Horned Larks are drab, brown birds with 'batman' head markings: two small, black horns (seldom visible), black sideburns and a black breast blotch. Their black tail is obvious in flight. Sky Larks resemble large, streaked sparrows with a slight head crest. They have white outer tail feathers.

Horned Lark: *adult*

'Don't fence me in' could be the theme song for Horned Larks. The only native species of the lark family found in North America, Horned Larks have a love for wide open spaces, from the alpine to the Arctic.

These ground nesters have adapted to some degree to agricultural areas. In winter Horned Larks form large flocks. They are almost invisible until something disturbs them; then they rise in a swirling mass, their black tails serving as an unmistakable field mark.

While most birds perch to sing, larks perform aerial displays almost out of sight in the sky, singing all the while. Their grand finale is to fold their wings and plummet to earth, only to pull out of their free-fall at the very last second. Once the lark has landed, the magic disappears; it then appears as rather unremarkable ground bird.

Sky Larks were introduced in the early 1900s to Vancouver Island. In spring these larks tinkle and trill high in the sky above the grassy fields they use for nesting. Although never numerous, they are year-round residents in open areas, where they scratch out a living with their pointed bills and elongated hind claws.

Sky Lark: *adult*

Seasonal Occurrence & Local Range: *Horned Larks can be seen on migration and in winter, when small flocks forage in open habitats along the seashore. They are most easily found in summer in alpine meadows. Sky Larks are localized year-round on southern Vancouver Island and in the San Juans.* **Size**: *Horned Lark: about 20 cm (8 in.); Sky Lark: about 18 cm (7 in.).*

AMERICAN PIPIT

Anthus rubescens

The American Pipit has a streaked, sparrow-like appearance (although the bill is thinner), with a buff breast, dark legs and a long tail with white outer feathers. It walks rather than hops and is often found alongside water, hence its former name, 'Water Pipit.'

American Pipit: *breeding*

American Pipits resemble sparrows, but they have a style all their own. In summer these alpine hikers stride along jauntily, swinging their tails after the fashion of their old-world relatives the 'wagtails.' Nonetheless, they are easy to overlook as they march over frosty hummocks or pause to peck at seeds or ground-dwelling insects. If startled, they bound up into the air, their white tail feathers conspicuous markers, until they land once more and tuck the feathers away. *Pip-it!* is the call these pipits make when flushed, and it is often a good first clue to their presence.

Because American Pipits are high country breeders, they often establish their territories while the snow still lingers. The nest is simply a scrape in the ground in a bit of a hollow, away from the blasting wind. When the male American Pipit is courting, he sails high through the sky, then flutters slowly back to the ground, like a parachutist. After breeding and rearing their young, the pipits leave their summer alpine homes to spend winter at the seashore.

Seasonal Occurrence & Local Range: *After breeding, American Pipits migrate down in latitude and elevation to winter in fields and lowland farms near the coast. They overwinter from southern B.C. southwards. They are most common in our area during migration in April and September.*
Size: *about 15 cm (6 in.).*

🌲 WINTER WREN
Trogolodytes trogolodytes

Wrens are small, brown birds with slender bills. A Winter Wren is a tiny, dark bird with a stubby tail and barred wings, tail and belly. It constantly bobs and teeters as it secretively flits about the dense undergrowth.

Winter Wren: *adult*

From the cool, shady, temperate rain forests of the West Coast, a loud, bubbling song rises and falls incessantly. Like little opera singers, Winter Wrens boldly announce their claim to a chunk of woodland, where they make their home in the overturned roots of fallen trees or under the bank near a stream. The Latin name *trogolodytes* means, literally, 'one who creeps into holes' and is often translated as 'cave dweller' as well.

The energetic and sometimes polygamous male makes several rough nests from which the female chooses one to 'furnish' with feathers and soft grasses. She alone incubates the young, the male sleeping in a nest of his own. However, despite these separate living arrangements, he helps feed and care for his family.

As the temperatures drop, Winter Wrens cluster together for warmth, occasionally in large numbers. One icy, winter evening, 46 wrens were found piled three layers deep in a single nesting box.

These tough, little wrens are so well adapted to northern climes that they are found throughout Europe and Asia, including the Himalayas. In fact, this species is 'the wren' of English-speaking Europe.

Seasonal Occurrence & Local Range: *Winter Wrens are year-round residents along the coast. They are most abundant fall through winter, when birds move down from higher elevations or from further north and take up residence in shady, urban gardens.*
Size: *about 10 cm (4 in.).*

LARGER WRENS 🌲 🦅

HOUSE WREN
Troglodytes aedon

BEWICK'S WREN
Thryomanes bewickii

The House Wren is plain brown, with a faint eye-ring lacking a sharp eye stripe. Bewick's Wren has a bold, white eyebrow stripe, brown back and whitish underparts. Note the latter's long tail (with white outer tail feathers), which it holds cocked and flits sideways. Bewick's are the largest of the West Coast wrens.

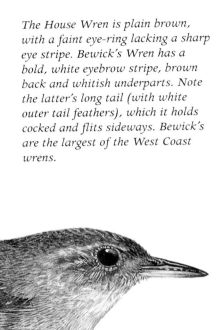

House Wren: *adult*

The House Wren's cheery song and energetic demeanor make it a welcome addition to any neighborhood, where it will eagerly nest in man-made boxes. The female alone incubates the eggs, but the male feeds his partner and keeps an eye on the nest site.

Wrens often sing from under cover but occasionally they let loose in full view, allowing you to marvel at how such a little bird can produce such big sounds with tireless repetition. This singing stamina led one native group to name wrens 'a big noise for their size.' Unlike Winter Wrens, which tend to stay near the forest floor, House Wrens frequent the next level up in shrubs and trees.

A buzzy rasp followed by a series of sharp, clear notes is often the first clue to the presence of Bewick's Wrens. Perhaps a similarity of lifestyles accounts for the fact that there is very little tolerance between this species and House Wrens. However, unlike the summer-visiting House Wrens, Bewick's tend to be year-round residents, which perhaps gives them an advantage. On cold winter nights, Bewick's Wrens huddle in nest boxes or on a wires next to a house, attempting to stay warm.

Bewick's Wren: *adult*

Seasonal Occurrence & Local Range: *The House Wrens' summer range does not extend much north of mid-Vancouver Island and the Sunshine Coast. They are absent from the B.C. Lower Mainland. Bewick's Wrens are found north to mid-Vancouver Island and southern coastal B.C. These year-round residents are the most common wren of the San Juans and the Seattle region.* **Size**: *House: about 11 cm (4.5 in.); Bewick's: about 14 cm (5.5 in.).*

MARSH WREN

Cistothorus palustris

Marsh Wrens are predictably found where there are cattail and bulrush marshes, except during migration, when they may wander into other habitats. These wrens have white stripes on their brown back as well as a white eye stripe.

Marsh Wren: *adult*

You'll know Marsh Wrens are around if you are near a marsh and you hear a loud, rattling chatter, but getting a good look at them is another matter. Their call has often been likened to the sound of an old-fashioned sewing machine.

Marsh Wrens seem to have an overabundance of energy. In spring the males may make up to 20 nests, which serve as dummy nest decoys to would-be predators and demonstrate the males' vigor and desirability to females. Oddly enough, although the female may choose her mate based on his prowess as a builder, she will lay her eggs only in a nest of her own making.

Marsh Wrens are not only defensive of their nests, they are extremely aggressive and will destroy the eggs of much larger marsh-dwelling birds such as Red-winged and Yellow-headed Blackbirds—as if to eliminate the competition.

If a male Marsh Wren has control over an especially productive piece of habitat, he will try to find a second mate and raise another family concurrently.

Seasonal Occurrence & Local Range: *In British Columbia, Marsh Wrens are widespread in marshes in summer but restricted to the south in winter. They are found year-round in coastal Washington and Oregon.*
Size: *about 13 cm (5 in.).*

AMERICAN DIPPER

Cinclus mexicanus

There is only one dipper species in North America—a plump, slate-gray bird with a jaunty, cocked tail. It has a habit of constantly doing deep knee bends and jumping into swiftly flowing streams.

American Dipper: *adult*

Swift streams and rivers provide food and lodging for American Dippers. They nest in mossy balls behind waterfalls or tuck their nests in streamside niches. Their food, on the other hand, lives on stream bottoms. Dippers plunge through the current, where they run along the river bed, swimming with their wings and foraging for fish eggs or the aquatic larvae of such insects as mayflies, caddisflies and stoneflies.

Dippers are almost always spotted bobbing on the rocks of a fast flowing stream or glimpsed flying with whirring wing beats low above the water. Their song is loud and ringing, intended to be heard above the roar of rivers and the babbling of brooks. In many ways, these birds look and behave like plump, gray, semi-aquatic wrens.

Ice and snow are no deterrent to these wonderfully adapted 'water ouzels,' as the British call them. Only if their rivers freeze over do they leave, flying down in elevation to the nearest open water.

Seasonal Occurrence & Local Range: *American Dippers are year-round residents all along the coast where there are rushing streams and rivers. There is some elevational migration in cold weather.*
Size: *about 18 cm (7 in.).*

KINGLETS 🌲

GOLDEN-CROWNED KINGLET
Regulus satrapa

RUBY-CROWNED KINGLET
Regulus calendula

The Golden-crowned Kinglet is a small, olive-green bird with a white eye stripe. The female's crown is yellow, and the male's is golden-orange. Only the male Ruby-crowned Kinglet has a ruby crown; the gray-olive female lacks a crown patch. The broken, white eye-ring of the 'Ruby-crown' is distinctive.

male

female

Golden-crowned Kinglet: *adults*

Kinglets are olive-drab birds, smaller and plumper than warblers, with slender bills and a double wing bar. Golden-crowned Kinglets are generally heard before they are seen, although their lisping *see-see-see* sounds are at the upper range of most human hearing.

Kinglets flit restlessly, high in the tops of conifer trees, constantly flicking their wings as they glean insects. Their acrobatic feeding style and preference for treetops make it a challenge to glimpse their colorful crowns. Golden-crowned Kinglets often associate with mixed flocks of chickadees and nuthatches, especially in winter.

The Ruby-crowned Kinglet has a long, rolling song that sounds like this little bird is exuberantly trying to attract attention: *tee, tee, tee, tew, tew, tew, look at Me, look at Me, look at Me!* Male Ruby-crowns often keep their brightly colored caps concealed, but when they are excited, they raise their crown feathers in an impressive display of red.

Hutton's Vireos, which are uncommon year-round residents, resemble Ruby-crowns but are larger and more sluggish looking, with a heavier bill and broken eye-ring.

female

male

Ruby-crowned Kinglet: *adults*

Seasonal Occurrence & Local Range: *Golden-crowned Kinglets flourish year-round in coniferous forests all along the West Coast. Ruby-crowns are year-round residents, although they are most often seen on migration, when large numbers of nonresidents pass through.*
Size: *Golden: about 9 cm (3.5 in.); Ruby: about 10 cm (4 in.).*

GRAY CATBIRD

Dumetella carolinensis

The Gray Catbird is a slate gray, robin-sized bird with a black crown, and rusty feathers on the underside of the base of the tail. This bird often flips its tail and holds it at an upturned angle.

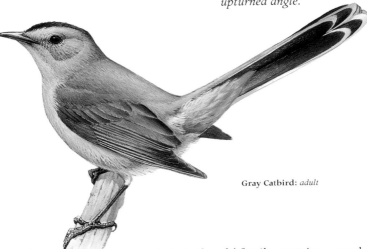

Gray Catbird: *adult*

Further east and south, the 'mimic thrush' family contains a number of interesting birds with names like 'thrasher' and 'mockingbird.' Along the Pacific Northwest Coast, the only mimic thrush is the Gray Catbird, and it does the family proud. True to its name, this species has a call that sounds an awful lot like a mewing cat, but it spoils the impersonation by working in phrases that sound like rusty gate hinges, and mimicking birds songs. As well, the catbird is one of the few birds in our area that regularly sings at night.

Gray Catbirds prefer dense vegetation, and often they can be difficult to see in their preferred habitats of underbrush and densely planted gardens, where they eat mostly insects and fruit. During nesting season, the male does most of the provisioning of the young, while the female stays on the nest. The female's faithfulness to the nest is one reason why these catbirds are not very susceptible to parasitism by Brown-headed Cowbirds. The female cowbird has trouble sneaking her egg into the catbird nest, and even if she succeeds, mother catbirds are good at recognizing the odd eggs and ejecting them.

Seasonal Occurrence & Range: *Gray Catbirds are rare and localized in our area; they are almost always seen in summer.*
Size: *about 23 cm (9 in.).*

NORTHERN SHRIKE

Lanius excubitor

Northern Shrikes are medium-sized, gray birds with a slightly hooked bill and a black mask over the eyes. The wings and tail are black. They have an undulating style of flight in which they show off contrasting black, white and gray areas. Juvenile Northern Shrikes are brownish.

Northern Shrike: *adult*

Shrikes are songbirds that hunt other birds yet manage without the usual weapons. Lacking the talons of raptors and the advantage of size, they seize their prey with their powerful, hooked bill, often crushing the prey's neck vertebrae. Of course, smaller prey are easier for them to handle.

On the breeding grounds, the males skewer their prey on a hawthorn bush or a string of barbed wire to impress females. Shrikes are sometimes called 'butcher birds,' since they often have favorite locations where they shishkabob their meals. The shrikes' black bandit eye stripe adds to their slightly sinister aura.

Northern Shrikes are usually seen in open country, perched on a wire or shrub, waiting for a bird, mouse or cricket to catch their eye. They have a distinctive, upright silhouette that is easy to recognize with practice. In winter their usual call is a buzzy note, but when spring comes around, they can be quite musical in the days before they head north to breed.

Seasonal Occurrence & Local Range: *True to their name, Northern Shrikes summer far north in B.C., Alaska and the Yukon, west to the Aleutians. In winter they are seen in semi-open habitat south to California.*
Size: *about 25 cm (10 in.).*

173

WAXWINGS

CEDAR WAXWING 🌲
Bombycilla cedrorum

BOHEMIAN WAXWING
Bombycilla garrulus

Cedar Waxwings are smooth-looking, crested birds with a black mask, waxy red wing-tips and yellow-tipped tail. Bohemian Waxwings are almost identical but larger, with white wing patches and rusty rather than white under the tail.

Cedar Waxwing: *adult*

Cedar Waxwings don't seem to have any particular preference for cedar trees, but they do secrete a red substance at the tips of their secondary wing feathers in a line of tiny drops that resemble blobs of sealing wax. Researchers recently discovered that pigments from the berries the birds eat contribute to the production of the red color.

In late summer and fall, these handsome birds flock together to gorge on berries. When their crops are full and they can eat no more, they continue picking fruit and pass it down the line like a bucket brigade, until finally one bird gulps the berry down. If the berries have fermented, the wax-wings will show definite signs of tipsiness, flying erratically and flopping around on the ground.

Cedar Waxwings whisper back and forth between themselves constantly. Their call is a soft quavering *ssee-ssee-ssee*. It's worth getting to know this sound because unless you hear them first, these subtle beauties are easy to overlook.

Bohemian Waxwings are the northern equivalent to the Cedars, and you should double-check every winter waxwing to be sure of its species identity.

Seasonal Occurrence & Local Range: *Cedar Waxwings are widespread breeders along the coast in summer. They winter south, ranging north irregularly to southern B.C. in search of fruits and berries. Bohemians nest in the B.C. Coast Range, and occasionally, roving bands make an appearance in winter.*
Size: *Cedar: about 18 cm (7 in.); Bohemian: about 20 cm (8 in.).*

174

STARLING FAMILY BIRDS

 **EUROPEAN STARLING**
Sturnus vulgaris

CRESTED MYNA
Acridotheres cristatellus

Our two members of the starling family resemble short-tailed blackbirds; they can be identified in flight by their tailless, triangular silhouette. In spring European Starlings gleam with iridescent blues and greens accented with a sharp, yellow bill. In winter their feathers are speckled. Crested Mynas have a tuft of feathers at the base of their bill, and in flight they flash large, white wing patches.

European Starling: *breeding*

Members of the starling family are good-looking birds with glossy feathers and a talent for mimicry. European Starlings and Crested Mynas, the two West Coast representatives, are both introduced species. Their arrival was mixed news for native birds—the starling has caused some indigenous species to decline, whereas the myna has carved out a tiny niche of its own.

The people who first introduced starlings to North America were thinking of literature rather than ecology. They wanted all the birds from Shakespeare's works to be living in New York so that new immigrants would feel more at home. Now the super-successful starlings are causing the demise of some native birds and are also outcompeting the mynas, which were introduced from their native Southeast Asia to Vancouver in 1897.

On cold days, mynas and starlings hang around chimneys, like hobos warming themselves at a fire. Crested Mynas are seen most often near reliable sources of urban garbage such as fast food outlets and grocery stores. Because their only North American home is Vancouver, many birders make special trips there to try to see them.

Seasonal Occurrence & Local Range: *European Starlings are widespread, year-round residents. They are especially numerous near human habitations. Only a few hundred Crested Mynas survive in Vancouver, staying there year-round.*
Size: *Starling: about 20 cm (8 in.); Myna: about 27 cm (10.5 in.).*

175

NORTHWESTERN CROW

Corvus caurinus

AMERICAN CROW

Corvus brachyrhynchos

Crows are distinguished by their solid black color and their sharp, all-purpose beaks. In flight crows can be distinguished from ravens by their tails, which are squared off rather than spade shaped.

Northwestern Crow: *adult*

Northwestern Crows are the West Coast equivalent of the widespread American Crow. In fact, some ornithologists believe they are simply two geographic races within the same species.

At low tide Northwestern Crows can be seen walking the beach, flipping over sticks and shreds of sea lettuce as they search for tasty morsels. These brainy birds are known to hide bits of their booty above the high tide line for later and to open clams by dropping them onto roads or allowing cars to drive over them.

Although these crows often tend to organize their day around low tide, they are resourceful and demonstrate versatility when it comes to finding alternate food sources, depending on what happens to be the speciality of the season. In spring at nesting time, they can be seen sneaking around searching for other birds' babies or lurking quietly, watching for other birds to reveal the whereabouts of their nests. Almost any time of year they can be found competing with human scavengers as they dumpster-dive for scraps in town.

In fall Northwestern Crows form flocks and roost together. As night thickens, black banners of crows stream across the sky en route to their communal sleeping spots.

Seasonal Occurrence & Local Range: *The Northwestern Crow is a year-round resident whose range extends from Washington to Alaska and inland to around Hope in British Columbia. In Washington they intergrade with American Crows.*
Size: *about 41 cm (16 in.).*

COMMON RAVEN

Corvus corax

Ravens are larger than their crow relatives. When seen in profile, they show a ruffle of breast feathers at the throat called a goiter patch, and a much stouter bill. In flight their tail is spade shaped.

Common Raven: *adult*

In coastal native lore, Raven is aptly named 'the trickster' for his clever ways. His loud croaking is like a raucous laugh—he seems to be guffawing at a joke, undoubtedly one at someone else's expense. At other times, a raven will seem to be talking to itself, mixing croaks, gurgles and bill claps in an ever-entertaining patter of avian rumblings.

Adult Common Ravens form strong pair bonds that last for life. Their courtship behaviors rival any air show acrobatics: they lock feet and fall together, barrel rolling and tumbling through space, breaking their embrace at the last possible second.

Couples patrol their territories, eking out a living under severe conditions in extreme environments. During the hunting season, ravens often trail after hunters looking to score an easy meal. Long after most other birds have fled south or down to milder valleys, ravens remain lords of the high country—often surviving on other animals that have succumbed to the rigors of winter. Young ravens roost together at night, collaborating to find food and to compete with the well-established adult couples.

Seasonal Occurrence & Local Range: *Common Ravens are extremely versatile year-round residents, ranging from the mountains to the sea.* **Size**: *about 61 cm (24 in.).*

GRAY JAY
Perisoreus canadensis

These rather tame, small-billed members of the jay and crow family are pale gray with a darker nape and back. The immatures are dark sooty gray all over. Gray Jays do not have a crested head.

Gray Jay: *adult*

The Gray Jay is a phantom of higher elevation forests. As any hiker or skier knows, when you sit down to a picnic lunch, a band of Gray Jays will magically materialize. These uninvited guests return repeatedly to beg for morsels, then disappear to stash their food for another rainy or snowy day. Gray Jays cement their snacks to a tree trunk using their own saliva. This hoarding behavior helps the bird get through lean times or severe winter weather and is an alternative to migration.

Gray Jays begin nesting when the snow is still deep, so they insulate their nests with bark, grass, fur and other warm materials—which no doubt helps keep both the eggs and the parent birds warm. At this time of year, the only other nesting birds are likely to be Great Horned Owls.

Gray Jays go by a number of names, from Canada Jay, to Whiskey Jack, to the not-so-flattering 'Camp Robber,' in recognition of their pilfering tendencies. These birds' hoarding habits are enshrined in their scientific name, *Perisoreus canadensis*, which means something like 'the Canadian heaper-upper.'

Seasonal Occurrence & Local Range: *Gray Jays are forest-dwelling birds of the Coast Mountains and Cascades. They are common visitors to feeders in appropriate locations, such as most ski resort towns.*
Size: *about 29 cm (11.5 in.).*

BLUISH JAYS

 **STELLER'S JAY**
Cyanocitta stelleri

WESTERN SCRUB-JAY
Aphelocoma californica

The dark-crested Steller's Jay looks almost black until the light picks up the velvet blue colors of its wings, breast and tail. It raises or lowers its crest to reflect its relative state of agitation. The Western Scrub-Jay is a crestless, blue jay with a white throat and brown back.

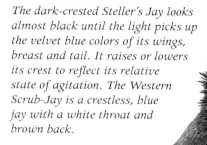

Steller's Jay: *adult*

Steller's Jays, the provincial bird of British Columbia, are the western counterparts of the eastern Blue Jay. These year-round residents live on forest slopes among evergreens.

Announcing their arrival with a raucous *shack-shack-shack,* Steller's Jays descend upon bird feeders, scattering smaller birds like a local street gang. With their dark, velvety blue feathers and handsome head crest, Steller's Jays make up in good looks for whatever they may lack in manners. Despite their habits, most people who feed birds are happy to have them drop by.

Their large feet are ill-suited for grasping small perches, so Steller's Jays on a feeder intended for smaller species hang precariously and eat greedily until they can hang on no longer. In the end, they do the ground feeders a favor by strewing seeds widely as they messily stuff their beaks.

Western Scrub-Jays are common in Oregon but very rare further north in the West Coast area. They are usually found near oak forests and behave in typical rowdy jay style.

Seasonal Occurrence & Local Range: *Steller's Jays range from Alaska southwards. Winter dispersal of interior birds can greatly augment coastal populations in the fall and winter. Western Scrub-Jays are common in Oregon but extremely rare farther north.*
Size: *Steller's Jay: about 30 cm (12 in.); Scrub-Jay: about 28 cm (11 in.).*

179

CLARK'S NUTCRACKER
Nucifraga columbiana

A Clark's Nutcracker could be mistaken for a Gray Jay, but its bold white patches on black wings, and white edges on a short, black tail are especially noticeable in flight. The nutcracker's loud, grating kra-aah! *call makes a lasting impression.*

Clark's Nutcracker: *adult*

Clark's Nutcrackers are very habitat-specific birds. You can expect to see them where whitebark pine trees grow in rocky areas near the timberline. These members of the crow family have a longish, sharply pointed, black bill that looks very similar to a flicker's but is designed for prying seeds from the pinecones on which it specializes.

While food-caching behavior is common amongst their crow, magpie and jay relatives, the nutcrackers out-perform them all, stashing 30,000 to 100,000 seeds in a single autumn season. Clark's Nutcrackers have an extraordinary ability to remember where they hid the seeds months afterwards. This behavior ensures the birds have a reliable food source in the depths of winter, and the seeds that are not recovered will occasionally sprout, thus benefiting the tree as well. Scientists have tested the memories of Clark's Nutcrackers against those of graduate students, and the nutcrackers invariably win.

On occasion, Clark's Nutcrackers become almost as tame as Gray Jays, and at a casual glance they look a lot alike. However, the nutcracker is always a 'wilder' bird and, in most people's eyes, more exciting as well.

Seasonal Occurrence & Local Range: *These year-round residents of high altitude ridges and subalpine forests sometimes cruise downhill in winter in search of gentler weather, or to visit ski areas, where they seek out unnatural additions to their diet.*
Size: *about 30 cm (12 in.).*

BUSHTIT
Psaltriparus minimus

Bushtits look like what they are: smaller, all gray, longer-tailed relatives of chickadees. Always gregarious, they flit through urban shrubbery in large flocks, often associating with their chickadee and kinglet neighbors. If you look closely, you'll notice that some Bushtits are pale-eyed—these are the females. West Coast Bushtits show a brownish crown.

Bushtit: *female*

Bushtits are master weavers who create long, sock-like nests with a tiny, round opening near the top. These nests are elaborate affairs of mosses, lichens, grasses and leaves woven together with spider webs around twigs for support, then lined with feathers and plant down. It may take a pair six weeks to build its love nest, but once it is done, the couple moves in, sleeping together and sharing the responsibilities of raising its family.

Bushtit families band together in the fall, sleeping huddled together for warmth on cold, winter nights. By day the birds trickle through the shrubbery and deciduous woodlands, constantly calling in high, lisping voices to maintain contact.

For many birders, the Bushtit is one of those right-under-your-nose discoveries that makes birding such an eye-opening pastime.

Seasonal Occurrence & Local Range: *Bushtits do not extend far north beyond the southern suburban areas of mainland B.C. and southern Vancouver Island. They are found mostly west of the Cascades and are common residents in hedgerows and around towns in Washington, including the San Juans.*
Size: *about 11 cm (4.5 in.).*

CHICKADEES

BLACK-CAPPED CHICKADEE 🌲
Parus atricapillus

MOUNTAIN CHICKADEE
Parus gambeli

CHESTNUT-BACKED CHICKADEE
Parus rufescens
Pendev - c R

Chickadees are small birds with long, thin tails and dark heads. The Black-capped Chickadee sports a black cap and bib on an otherwise plain gray background. The Mountain Chickadee has a distinctive white eyebrow through its black cap. With its cedar-colored flank and back, the Chestnut-backed Chickadee is the most colorful local member of its family.

Black-capped Chickadee: *adult*

Chickadees descend in merry, little mobs to bird feeders, where they hang around to enjoy their meals. Seldom alone, they flit from tree to tree scouring the branches for insects, often hanging acrobatically upside down as they search for those tiny creatures that might evade them by hiding under twigs and leaves.

Mountain Chickadee: *adult*

In summer chickadees stash insects and seeds for tough times ahead. During the short, cold days of winter, these small birds must work hard to find enough food to survive the long nights. They seek out warm places to snuggle together amidst thick foliage or in a woodpecker's hole. Despite their small beaks, resourceful chickadees can also excavate their own holes.

Birders generally love chickadees for their cheery appearance, but these energetic flitters are also useful as a means of locating other birds. In fall listen for chickadees and then watch for mixed flocks of chickadees and migrating warblers. At any time of year, a scolding *dee-dee-dee* sound may signal a group of chickadees mobbing an owl.

Chestnut-backed Chickadee: *adult*

Seasonal Occurrence & Local Range: *The three species have distinct and different habitat preferences. Black-capped Chickadees live in deciduous and mixed woodlands. The Mountain Chickadee, a bird of interior coniferous forests, barely enters our region on the eastern edge. The Chestnut-backed Chickadee is found in coniferous forests and is the only chickadee found on Vancouver Island, where it is common in all treed habitats.*
Size: *all about 14 cm (5.5 in.).*

NUTHATCHES 🌲 🏔

RED-BREASTED NUTHATCH
Sitta canadensis

WHITE-BREASTED NUTHATCH
Sitta carolinensis

Nuthatches are small, short-tailed birds with sharp beaks. Red-breasted Nuthatches have a black cap with a white eye stripe, and a wash of rusty color on their chest. They forage from the top of a tree to the bottom, spiraling down the trunk headfirst, tweezing insects out of the bark with their sharp, thin bills. White-breasted Nut-hatches, who behave similarly, lack the rusty chest and white eye line.

Red-breasted Nuthatch: *male*

The nasal *yank, yank, yank* call of Red-breasted Nuthatches is a familiar sound of West Coast forests. Nuthatches form committed couples, sticking close to home year-round if there is enough food or a reliable bird feeder in their territory. Visiting their neighborhood bird feeder 'cafeteria' with great regularity, they dart in like little missiles, never lingering longer than it takes to grab a seed and dash off to eat it or stash it in seclusion.

Nuthatches are cavity-nesting birds, with lifestyles much like chickadees or miniature woodpeckers. When excavating a nest, their hammering can sound very much like a woodpecker, and the finished result looks much like a woodpecker hole.

White-breasted Nuthatches, which are similar but slightly larger, occur only rarely in western Washington and on Vancouver Island, preferring drier habitats where Garry oaks dominate. Their call, a chuckling *heh-heh-heh-heh*, is similar to the Red-breasted's *heh-heh*, but lower pitched, and it takes practice to recognize it in the field.

Seasonal Occurrence & Local Range: *These year-round residents do well wherever there are mature conifer or mixed conifer-deciduous forests.*
Size: *both about 11 cm (4.5 in.)*

BROWN CREEPER

Certhia americana

Brown Creepers combine the mottled brown, camouflage coloration and thin, decurved bill of a wren with the long, stiff tail feathers of a woodpecker. They typically forage upwards on tree bark, unlike nuthatches who will forage up, down or sideways. A white stripe above the eyes is visible in good light.

Brown Creeper: *adult*

The Brown Creeper is a common resident of West Coast forests. It is often overlooked because of its cryptic coloration and its furtive approach to life. Usually a moving flake of bark first catches your eye and gradually takes the shape of a bird. Intent on its feeding, the creeper spirals up large tree trunks, myopically plucking hidden invertebrate morsels from fissures in the bark with its tweezers-like bill. As it nears the treetop, the creeper drops to the base of a nearby tree to begin its grooming ascent all over again. When frightened, a Brown Creeper freezes and flattens itself against the tree trunk, becoming impossible to see.

The Brown Creeper's high and exuberant song has been described as *trees, trees, trees, see the trees,* which somehow seems fitting given this bird's lifestyle. In winter a single, high, thin note is all you will hear from this bird.

Seasonal Occurrence & Local Range: *Brown Creepers reside year-round along the coast as far north as Alaska, although they may withdraw to warmer climes or lower elevations in severe weather.*
Size: *about 13 cm (5 in.).*

AMERICAN ROBIN
Turdus migratorius

male

female

Like all thrushes, American Robins are medium-sized generalists with a remarkable singing talent. A brick-red breast, streaks on a white throat and a gray back distinguish robins. Young birds resemble adults but have a spotted breast.

American Robin: *adults*

In March migrating American Robins arrive in flocks, then begin disputing their territories in the happiest ways. Their jaunty *cheerily-cheery-up cheery-o* is a sure sign that spring must soon follow. Meanwhile, the large flocks of robins that have overwintered in our region on a diet of fruit and berries often carry on further north to breed.

If you walk through woodlands, a robin may burst from the bushes with hysterical chirping, as if certain of your ill-intentions. This behavior is much more typical of thrushes than the casual attitudes that suburban birds show towards humans.

The familiar sight of a robin standing on the lawn with one ear cocked towards the earth is not, as some would have you believe, the act of listening for worms. The bird is actually watching and searching for worm movements.

For many, the discovery of a robin's nest with its four perfect, blue eggs is an early childhood memory. Robins make up part of the emotional land-scape of coastal communities—with their song, their young's hatching and their deaths.

Seasonal Occurrence & Local Range: *Robins are seen year-round in our area. The summer birds retreat further south in fall and are replaced by northern breeders, giving a false impression of residency. Robins do well in suburbia, forest borders and open woods.*
Size: *about 23 cm (9 in.).*

 **VARIED THRUSH**

Ixoreus naevius

This elegant thrush resembles a robin with a black band across the breast. Orange in the wings and an orange eye stripe also set it apart.

Varied Thrush: *male*

Like a duet warming up, the Varied Thrush hums and whistles single, long notes, first at one pitch, then higher or lower. This lovely sound, wafting from the darkness of misty conifers, opens and closes damp spring days.

Sometimes, overcome by spring fever, the Varied Thrush forgets its secretive nature and perches boldly on roadsides or conspicuously in trees. Here it will sing throughout the day and provide birders the opportunity to admire its sophisticated markings. At times you will even see this bird in the company of American Robins, hunting worms on a lawn.

Varied Thrushes are most commonly seen during migration and in winter. When storms blanket the coastal ranges, these shy birds infiltrate urban gardens in search of fruit from ornamentals or seeds from backyard feeders. However, when the coolest winter days have passed, most Varied Thrushes regain their dignified place in the moist woodlands, proclaiming spring with a song that cuts through the heavy air. Some follow the retreating snowline up the mountains; others move further north.

Seasonal Occurrence & Local Range: *These residents of deep coniferous forests migrate vertically, moving up the mountains in summer and down again in winter.*
Size: *about 25 cm (10 in.).*

187

SWAINSON'S THRUSH 🌲 🐾
Catharus ustulatus

The Swainson's is a spotted thrush with a light eye-ring, tawny color beneath the breast spots and an olive-brown back.

Swainson's Thrush: *adult*

Beauty in forest birds is often gauged by sound and not sight. Given this criterion, the thrushes are among the loveliest of birds. The flute-like notes of the Swainson's Thrush spiral upwards in a question that lingers in the coastal forest air. In spring Swainson's Thrushes query into the evening, long after other birds have called it a day. Also conspicuous is their impatient call note, a crisp *what?*

A migrant to the coastal rain forests, Swainson's Thrushes are frequently heard but rarely seen during their brief four month stay in evergreen and damp mixed forests. They reveal themselves only when flocking together for their passage south to Central and South America.

Like all songbirds, thrushes stop to feed by day and migrate under the cover of darkness. In September large flocks of Swainson's Thrushes pass over our heads at night, navigating by the stars with pinpoint precision.

Seasonal Occurrence & Local Range: *The first Swainson's Thrushes of spring arrive in May; they depart again by early October. Their songs enliven moist forests below 1000 meters (about 3300 feet).*
Size: *about 18 cm (7 in.).*

HERMIT THRUSH
Catharus guttatus

The Hermit is a spot-breasted, rufous-tailed thrush that flips its wings and lifts its tail, then slowly lowers it when perched.

Hermit Thrush: *adult*

The song of the Hermit Thrush is a reward to hikers who venture into this thrush's mountain environments. Like a jazz improvisation, the flute-like notes rise and fall, each series of notes beginning with a clear whistle at a different pitch.

This exquisite song inspired many to write of it, including Walt Whitman and Abraham Lincoln. A Hermit Thrush caroling at dusk moved the great naturalist John Burroughs to write, 'Listening to this strain on the lone mountain, with the full moon just rounded on the horizon, the pomp of your cities and the pride of your civilization seemed trivial and cheap.'

This 'shy and hidden' bird may briefly treat early spring coastal campers to its evensong before it moves into higher elevation forests to nest. The Hermit is the only thrush in the genus *Catharus* (the brown thrushes, as opposed to the robins and Varied Thrush) that occasionally lingers through the winter in Oregon, Washington and southern British Columbia where lowland areas provide adequate fruits and berries.

Seasonal Occurrence & Local Range: *Hermit Thrushes summer above 1000 meters (about 3300 feet) all along the coast. A few winter on the southern end of Vancouver Island and the San Juans, and from the south coast of B.C. through coastal Washington.*
Size: *about 18 cm (7 in.).*

EYE-STRIPED VIREOS 🌲

RED-EYED VIREO
Vireo olivaceus

WARBLING VIREO
Vireo gilvus

Vireos resemble large, sluggish, olive-yellow warblers with a heavier bill. Red-eyed Vireos have a red eye, a white eye stripe bordered with black, and a gray cap. Warbling Vireos are very plain with a faint, whitish eye stripe lacking borders. They are more overall gray than olive in color.

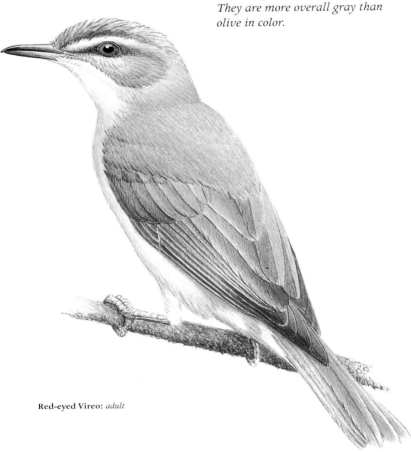

Red-eyed Vireo: *adult*

Vireos' olive-yellow coloration provides them with excellent camouflage in trees and shrubs, where they glean their food off the foliage. It is best to try to get to know their songs because they can be very difficult to see.

From deciduous forests and streamside shrubbery comes the incessant summer song of the Red-eyed Vireo. Vireos are singing endurance champions, and one patient researcher calculated that this tireless performer sings its song up to 10,000 times a day. Sounding like a robin who is practicing elocution, this bird articulates each phrase distinctly and separately: *look-up, way-up, tree-top see-me, here-I am*. Taken literally, this is much easier said than done.

Warbling Vireos are nondescript birds that frequent the tip-tops of deciduous trees. Their rambling song wafts down, sounding like a Purple Finch with a touch of laryngitis.

Warbling Vireo: *adult*

Seasonal Occurrence & Local Range: *Red-eyed Vireos migrate from South America to breed in southwestern B.C., but in Washington they are most common in the east. Warbling Vireos are common summer breeders ranging all along the coast.*
Size: *Red-eyed: about 15 cm (6 in.); Warbling: about 13 cm (5 in.).*

SPECTACLED VIREOS 🌲

SOLITARY VIREO
Vireo solitarius

HUTTON'S VIREO
Vireo huttoni

The Solitary Vireo has a gray head with bold, white spectacles, and broad double wing bars on a drab, greenish body. Hutton's Vireo is olive green with a fainter eye-ring that does not quite close over top of the eye, and broad double wing bars.

Solitary Vireo: *adult*

The Solitary Vireo sounds like it's talking to itself. It repeatedly warbles a question, then an answer: *vreeip? vreeip!* Despite its loud song, it is frustratingly difficult to get a good look at this bird because it frequents the treetops of the forests where it breeds.

Of all the vireos, Hutton's Vireo is the only resident vireo species on the coast. In winter it often associates with the kinglets it resembles. The Hutton's looks like a large, laid-back Ruby-crowned Kinglet that doesn't flick its wings. In March and April, and then again a bit in August, the Hutton's sings a monotonous series of *zu-wheeps*.

Because vireos feed on leaf-eating insects, they act as natural pest control agents. Chemical pesticides not only deprive them of their natural food source, but also can poison these helpful birds.

Hutton's Vireo: *adult*

Seasonal Occurrence & Local Range: *From April through September the Solitary Vireo is a common breeder in a wide variety of forest types in Washington and southern B.C., and on Vancouver Island. Hutton's is a year-round resident along the coast of Washington, on Vancouver Island and on B.C.'s north and central coast.*
Size: *Solitary: about 13 cm (5 in.); Hutton's: about 11 cm (4.5 in.).*

YELLOW-RUMPED 🌲 WARBLER

Dendroica coronata

Warblers are small, active, thin-beaked birds, usually with some yellow color. Yellow-rumped Warblers have blue-gray plumage with four distinct patches of yellow—on the rump, shoulders, cap and throat. Females and fall males have a faded look but have the same yellow patches.

female

male

Yellow-rumped Warbler: *breeding*

One of the most common wood warblers of the Pacific Northwest, the Yellow-rumped constantly flits between conifers and deciduous trees. It tends to favor the lower branches of trees, which helps the birdwatcher get a good look at the bird's boldly contrasting colors without cricking his or her neck. The Yellow-rumped's loud, two-part trill *seet-seet-seet-seet trrrrr* is synonymous with spring on the coast.

Yellow-rumpeds are versatile feeders. They glean insects from leaves, flycatch like swallows or flycatchers, and switch strategies as insects become available. Consequently, some Yellow-rumpeds can overwinter even when insects are scarce.

The Yellow-rumped Warbler represents a 'lumping' of two very similar subspecies—Audubon's Warbler (western) and the Myrtle Warbler (eastern), which are known to breed where their ranges overlap. The Audubon's Warbler has a yellow chin; the Myrtle's is white. Both forms migrate along the coast in spring and fall.

Seasonal Occurrence & Local Range: *Yellow-rumped Warblers are widespread breeders in summer. They winter from southern B.C. on down the coast, becoming increasingly common as one moves south.*
Size: *about 15 cm (6 in.).*

ORANGE-CROWNED WARBLER
Vermivora celata

This plain warbler is dull yellow with faint dark streaking on the breast. The orange crown feathers, for which it is named, are usually kept concealed.

female

male

Orange-crowned Warbler: *adults*

Don't bother looking for the orange crown, since you won't likely see it; this warbler's field markings are the lack thereof. Beginning birders find names like this one frustrating, but it is important to remember that the origin of many such bird names can be traced not to a birder with binoculars but to a museum ornithologist with a tray of study skins. In the hand, the orange crown may seem obvious, as could the white 'front' (forehead) of the Greater White-fronted Goose or the ring on the neck of the Ring-necked Duck. Then again, the specific name *celata* means concealed and refers to the usual status of the orange crown, so perhaps the specialists are toying with us after all.

Even the Orange-crowned's song is described as colorless—a single descending trill.

Orange-crowned Warblers have a sweet tooth and will sip nectar from flowers, visit sapsucker wells (the grid of holes they drill in tree bark to obtain sap and sap-feeding insects), or show up at hummingbird feeders.

Seasonal Occurrence & Local Range: *These hyperactive little warblers prefer deciduous areas and thickets, and are widespread and abundant along our coast from April through September.*
Size: *about 13 cm (5 in.).*

YELLOW WARBLER

Dendroica petechia

At a distance, these small birds appear to be bright yellow all over. Up close, the males are brighter than the females, and during the breeding season the males have fine, red streaks on their breast.

Yellow Warbler: *adults*

Although there's nothing common about their look, Yellow Warblers are commonly spotted along streamside woods and thickets in summer. This warbler is another one of those species that is often called a 'wild canary' by people who don't realize that there is no such thing in this part of the world. Few birds of our coast have the intense color of the Yellow Warbler or such a memorable courtship song: *sweet, sweet, sweet, I'm so-so sweet!* or *sweet, sweet shredded wheat!* A descending final note is often the distinctive part of a Yellow Warbler's song.

Although they are heavily parasitized by cowbirds, Yellow Warblers have evolved a variety of ways to elude these intruders. The warblers may abandon their nest and start again, or build another layer on their nest, on top of the offending egg as well as their own. One Yellow Warbler nest was found with six layers—a persistent defense but one that required a lot of egg laying!

Seasonal Occurrence & Local Range: *Yellow Warblers are summer breeders in our area, arriving with the rest of the songbirds later in the spring and migrating south in mixed flocks in fall.*
Size: *about 13 cm (5 in.).*

WILSON'S WARBLER
Wilsonia pusilla

Male Wilson's Warblers look like
Yellow Warblers at a glance, but
with a difference. The Wilson's has a
yellow breast, an olive-green back
and a neat, black skullcap. The
female is similar, but cap is more
subdued. Wilson's Warblers have a
restless habit of twitching their
wings and tail, much
like kinglets.

female

male

Wilson's Warbler: *adults*

Warblers (or, more properly, 'New World warblers' or 'wood warblers,'
since there is family of Old World warblers as well) have sometimes been
called the butterflies of the bird world because of their flamboyant breeding colors. Unlike butterflies, however, they are often secretive and difficult to get a good look at.

As well, when fall migration begins and many of these birds are in dull
nonbreeding or immature plumages, they can be difficult to tell apart,
particularly when they pass by in large, mixed-species flocks. At this time
of year, these birds are more like caterpillars—very difficult to identify
indeed. It is at this time that you come to appreciate the Wilson's Warbler,
one of the best looking and most distinctive examples of the group in any
season.

Wilson's Warblers glean insects in brushy areas including gardens. Their
song is an accelerating series of musical chips. They arrive en masse in
May, departing again in August to begin the long journey back to the
cloud forests of Central America.

Seasonal Occurrence & Local Range: *Wilson's Warblers range all along
the coast, nesting from sea level to the alpine. They are most abundant in
spring and again in August or September as the migratory waves pass
through.*
Size: *about 13 cm (5 in.).*

MACGILLIVRAY'S WARBLER

Oporornis tolmiei

This warbler has a gray hood, a partial white eye-ring on the top and bottom of the eye, a yellow breast and an olive back. Females are duller, as are males and immatures in the fall.

female

male

MacGillivray's Warbler: *adults*

The MacGillivray's Warbler is a secretive bird of streamside thickets and recently burned and disturbed areas at all altitudes. Listen for its five note song, often described as *sweeter-sweeter-sweeter, sugar-sugar.* The song drops on the last two notes.

This bird times its arrival from Central America and Mexico in spring to coincide with the emergence of leaves for concealment, and a burgeoning population of leaf-eating insects to feed on. It is a bird of the lower levels of the forest, unlike many of its treetop-dwelling warbler relatives.

The MacGillivray's is the western counterpart of the similar Mourning Warbler. Scientists speculate that these two originated from a common, hooded ancestor and were split by the division and rejoining of forest habitats during the ice ages that have dominated the recent geological history of this part of the world. These two species belong to the *Oporornis* group of warblers—they are easy to separate from the other warblers but difficult to distinguish from one another.

Seasonal Occurrence & Local Range: *MacGillivray's Warblers are widespread in our area where their brushy habitats, near avalanche tracks or streamside thickets, still exist. Like most other warblers, they arrive in May and begin southward migration by late summer.*
Size: *about 13 cm (5 in.).*

198

 COMMON YELLOWTHROAT
Geothlypis trichas

Common Yellowthroats have a typical warbler build, with a pointed bill and sleek contours. The lemon-yellow bib and 'Lone Ranger' eye mask easily identify the male. The female retains the lemon belly but lacks the eye mask. Both sexes are olive-brown above.

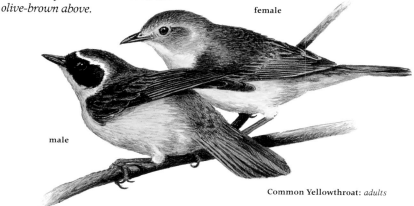

female

male

Common Yellowthroat: *adults*

Any shrubby area near water, and especially around cattail beds, is a likely place to listen for the oscillating *witchety-witchety-witchety* song of the Common Yellowthroat. Yellowthroats often remain well hidden in the undergrowth, leading birdwatchers on a merry chase of hide and seek. In breeding season, however, all coyness dissolves, and the male perches conspicuously to belt out his song and lay claim to his little patch of wetland.

The female Common Yellowthroat incubates alone, and the male helps bring home the grub, literally. Sometimes the family is raised without incident, but yellowthroats have the unfortunate distinction of being a prime target for nest-parasitizing cowbirds. Yellowthroats, like some other warblers, often contend with the interlopers by covering the alien egg in their nest with more nesting material and laying a second brood of eggs overtop.

This defense suggests that these two species have had a long history together and that the yellowthroats have evolved a method of reducing the impact of their freeloading neighbors—which some other birds have not.

Seasonal Occurrence & Local Range: *Common Yellowthroats are summer residents extending all along the coast and up into the mountains wherever there are pockets of wetland.*
Size: *about 11 cm (4.5 in.).*

OTHER WARBLERS 🌲 ⛰️

TOWNSEND'S WARBLER
Dendroica townsendi

**BLACK-THROATED GRAY
WARBLER**
Dendroica nigrescens

HERMIT WARBLER
Dendroica occidentalis

*Male Townsend's Warblers have a
striking head pattern that includes a
black ear patch bordered by yellow.
Their underparts are yellow, their
sides striped, and there are double
white bars on the wings. Females
Townsend's are similar, but they
have a greenish crown and ear patch.
The Black-throated Gray Warbler
has a similar plumage but with
white instead of yellow. Hermit
Warblers have a bright yellow face,
black bib and whitish underparts.*

male

female

Townsend's Warbler: *adults*

Learning the Townsend's wheezy song helps to detect its presence. *Zee-zee-
zee-ZEE-slick* is a common song interpretation. Easy to hear but hard to
see, these warblers forage near the tops of large conifers and seem to prefer
slightly higher elevations (above 600 meters [about 2000 feet]). Where there
are stands of old growth forest, however, Townsend's venture down to sea
level. They are the most common wood warbler of the Queen Charlotte
Islands. In the fall these flashy, little birds leave their conifer forests in the
highlands for their winter homes further south, where insects flourish.

The close relationship of the Townsend's and Black-throated Gray Warbler is obvious not only in their markings but also in the similarity of their songs. The Black-throated Gray, however, prefers mixed deciduous and conifer forests.

Within Washington, Townsend's is known to interbreed with the Hermit Warbler, a rain forest warbler whose range extends north only to the base of the Olympic Peninsula. The Hermit Warbler is a prize sighting for birdwatchers because it is so challenging to see. Spending most of its time in the very tip-tops of conifers, it can sometimes be lured lower by tape recordings of owls.

male

female

Black-throated Gray Warbler: *adults*

Seasonal Occurrence & Local Range: *All warblers are summer visitors. Townsend's typically breed in mountain conifer forests, but they range to sea level in the Queen Charlottes, San Juans and Gulf Islands. The Black-throated Gray Warbler's range extends midway up the B.C. coast and halfway up Vancouver Island. The Hermit Warbler is uncommon along the Washington coast in tall, coniferous forests.*
Size: *all about 10 cm (4 in.).*

COLORFUL MARSHLAND BLACKBIRDS

RED-WINGED BLACKBIRD
Agelaius phoeniceus

YELLOW-HEADED BLACKBIRD
Xanthocephalus xanthocephalus

Blackbirds are medium-sized, sharp-billed birds with a longer tail than the starlings. Red shoulder patches on a black background distinguish the male Red-winged Blackbird. Females resemble a large sparrow with streaky brown plumage and a pale eye stripe. Male Yellow-headed Blackbirds are black with a yellow head and a white patch in the wing. Females are reminiscent but duller.

male

female

Red-winged Blackbird: *adults*

In spring male Red-winged Blackbirds spar tirelessly. Their characteristic *kong-ka-REE!* song is the sound of battle as they vie for territory and females, flashing their crimson epaulets. *Ma-ma-MEE-ya* and *pull-the-LEE-ver!* are two more common attempts to render this classic sound onto the printed page.

Whichever male the females determine is the finest becomes the sultan of his patch of marsh, presiding over a harem of females all raising his offspring within his area of defended territory. After having been courted so glamorously, the females do all the work, weaving a nest amidst the stalks of bulrushes. The females' cryptic coloration enables them to sit like camouflaged corks on the nest, their streakiness blending perfectly with their surroundings.

Yellow-headed Blackbirds share the marsh habitat with the Red-winged and are just as colorful in their own way. Where both species occur, the larger, more aggressive Yellow-headed dominates, commandeering the center of the wetland and pushing the Red-winged Blackbirds to the periphery.

Seasonal Occurrence & Local Range: *Red-winged Blackbirds breed north to Alaska. In winter they retreat to southern British Columbia and points south. Yellow-headed Blackbirds show up during migration and occasionally linger over winter. They breed on Iona Island near Vancouver, the only coastal colony in the B.C. and Washington area.*
Size: *Red-winged: about 20 cm (8 in.); Yellow-headed: about 24 cm (9.5 in.).*

BREWER'S BLACKBIRD
Euphagus cyanocephalus

Brewer's Blackbirds are sharp-billed, long-tailed, all-dark birds. Males are black with a purplish sheen to the head, a purplish-green sheen to the body and a white eye. The females are brown with a dark eye.

male

female

Brewer's Blackbird: *adults*

Brewer's are the terrestrial counterparts to their marsh-loving relatives, and indeed, they look Red-winged Blackbirds without the bright red shoulder patches. Brewer's Blackbirds jerk their heads as they walk. This trait can be helpful in separating them from other members of the blackbird family, with which they form large flocks in winter. Fortunately for the beginning birder, the very similar Rusty Blackbird is rare in the Northwest Coast area.

Brewer's Blackbirds followed farmers north into Washington and B.C. around the turn of the century and, like cowbirds, make a living by feeding off the insects associated with livestock. Although they are most abundant around farmlands, it has become increasingly common to see them in winter hanging around civilized oases such as ski resorts, where they boldly scavenge whatever leavings they can find.

The call of a Brewer's Blackbird is thin and squealing, and in it you can hear the typical tonal quality of the songs of the blackbird group. Some blackbirds, like the Red-winged, make the most of this tone, but others, like the Brewer's, are about as musical as a rusty gate hinge.

Seasonal Occurrence & Local Range: *Brewer's Blackbirds extend midway up the coast of B.C. in summer and are found over all of Vancouver Island. They winter in southern B.C., Washington and Oregon, often in mixed flocks with other species of blackbirds.*
Size: *about 23 cm (9 in.).*

BROWN-HEADED COWBIRD

Molothrus ater

female

male

Brown-headed Cowbird: *adults*

The Brown-headed Cowbird is smaller than other blackbirds and has a stubbier bill; the male's chocolate brown head is its key field mark. The female looks like a nondescript, gray-brown finch.

The Brown-headed Cowbird's song, a bubbling *glug-ah-whee!*, might translate to other birds as 'here-comes-trouble!' We are told that the cowbirds historically followed the bison, feeding off the insects that associated with the huge herds. Since their food source was mobile, these birds devised a way of raising a family without having to settle down. By depositing an egg here and there in other birds' nests, they found they could depend on at least 200 other species to raise their offspring. In summer the female is an egg-laying machine able to deposit some 80 eggs in a succession of host nests.

Now no longer capable of making their own nest, cowbirds rely completely on other birds to raise their young. Cowbird eggs usually hatch before the host's eggs, and the cowbird chicks grow more rapidly and are typically larger than those of their hosts. The foster parents work incessantly feeding the over-sized and demanding cowbird chicks, while their own offspring may starve.

Cowbirds have expanded their range with deforestation and the clearing of land. They now prey upon species that had no previous contact with them and thus have added yet another pressure to songbirds that are struggling to survive owing to habitat loss.

Seasonal Occurrence & Local Range: *Brown-headed Cowbirds are ubiquitous along the West Coast during summer, particularly where man has altered the environment. Smaller populations remain on southern Vancouver Island and on the southern B.C. Mainland in winter, but most head further south.* **Size**: *about 18 cm (7 in.).*

WESTERN MEADOWLARK
Sturnella neglecta

The Western Meadowlark is camouflaged brown from the back and bright black and yellow from the front. Short, triangular wings and a short tail flanked with white on the edges give it a starling-like silhouette. A lemon-yellow breast with black V-neck set it apart, however.

Western Meadowlark: *adult*

Meadowlark songs are like cups full of music being poured from a pitcher. Once heard, they are not forgotten. These birds also tend to sing bird song dialects, so you will find that the songs of your local Western Meadowlarks are slightly different form those in other places—one of the subtleties that await the traveling birder.

Although meadowlarks have the sawed-off shape of a starling, they are a member of the blackbird group. The similarities result from convergent evolution.

From the back, Western Meadowlarks are nothing much to look at, and this works to their advantage. If they turn away and tuck in their white tail feathers, they become invisible against their grassland background, helpful when they are feeding or sitting on a nest. However, when they fly up from the ground and land on a perch facing you, their lemon-yellow breast is stunning.

Seasonal Occurrence & Local Range: *These birds of the grasslands are most common in the Interior, but they do show up along the coast, especially from September through April. They are uncommon, year-round residents in the San Juans and on Vancouver Island; in both areas their numbers have diminished. They are common in coastal Oregon.*
Size: *about 23 cm (9 in.).*

BULLOCK'S ORIOLE 🌲
Icterus bullockii

The male Bullock's Oriole is black-bird shaped but orange with a black crown, bib and eye stripe. Its big, white wing patches are also distinctive. The female is yellow with a white belly and gray back. Young males resemble their mother but have their father's black bib.

male

female

Bullock's Oriole: *adults*

Orioles are flamboyant orange and black relatives of blackbirds. In early spring female Bullock's Orioles sing too, a rather rare event in the bird world. A park where mature deciduous trees line the river is the most likely place to spot these orioles and their pendulous, swaying nests. Orioles tend to be loosely colonial, probably because their favored nesting habitat is in short supply.

Bullock's Oriole is replaced east of British Columbia and in the eastern U.S. by the Baltimore Oriole. Scientists have gone around in circles trying to decide if these birds are one species or two. They recently reversed their decision to lump the two species into one 'Northern Oriole' and so the 'Bullock's' is back. It is apparent that the two types of birds can and do interbreed where their ranges overlap, but in the best judgment of bird systematists, this interbreeding is not of the sort that might cause the two species to merge into one another.

The birds themselves, oblivious to their specific or subspecific status, fly back and forth between Mexico and their northern breeding grounds. Their greatest concern is adequate habitat and food.

Seasonal Occurrence & Local Range: *Bullock's Orioles are uncommon summer visitors west of the Cascades and Coast Mountains, but they are so spectacular that when one does show up you'll want to know what it is.*
Size: *about 20 cm (8 in.).*

WESTERN TANAGER
Piranga ludoviciana

Tanagers are medium-sized birds with medium-sized bills. The male Western Tanager is bright yellow with a black back and black wings. During the breeding season, the male's head is red. The female is paler yellow, but both sexes sport double wing bars and yellowish bills.

female

male

Western Tanager: *adults*

A male Western Tanager sighted in a West Coast mountain forest seems out of place. With his yellow body and 'dipped,' raspberry red head, he looks like the tropical bird that he is—at least for most of the year. As you go south from Canada, the tanager family becomes increasingly species-rich, until tanagers become some of the most abundant and obvious, colorful birds in the forests of South America.

Western Tanagers leave the tropics behind for a few months each spring to feast on the seasonal explosion of food in northern climes. After breeding, the male tanager's red head fades to yellow, which perhaps makes him less of a target during the perilous journey south.

The note of the tanager is a frog-like chirp, sometimes translated as *pit-a-peck,* and its song sounds something like an American Robin with a sore throat. Look for Western Tanagers in conifer trees and in mountain environments in summer. They can sometimes be lured to home feeders by putting out dried and fresh fruits on a tray.

Seasonal Occurrence & Local Range: *In summer Western Tanagers breed in coniferous trees north to Alaska, but in winter they retreat far south to Mexico and Central America. They are most common among Douglas-firs.* **Size:** *about 18 cm (7 in.).*

207

CROWNED SPARROWS

WHITE-CROWNED SPARROW
Zonotrichia leucophrys

**GOLDEN-CROWNED
SPARROW**
Zonotrichia atricapilla

Sparrows are small birds with subtle brown and gray plumages but with distinctive markings. The White-crowned is a gray sparrow with brown back and wings, and a white and black striped crown. The bill is pink or yellowish. Immatures have rusty brown crown stripes. Golden-crowned Sparrows resemble the White-crowned but have a yellow crown broadly banded with black. Immatures have only a faint yellow forehead on a brown crown.

White-crowned Sparrow: *adult*

Among a generally dull-looking lot that are sometimes dismissed as LBJs or 'little brown jobs,' the crowned sparrows are easy to distinguish. With their smooth, gray breast and smart-looking, white and black striped heads, White-crowned Sparrows always give an impression of being freshly turned out.

Sparrows are great singers, and their beautiful songs are a further aid to identification. Making up verbal descriptions of these songs can be quite entertaining. In spring White-crowned migrants insistently sing their utterly distinctive song, *I-I-I got-to-go wee-wee now!*, whereas local breeders typically belt out *zee-zee-zeetzi-dee-diddle-iddle-dee!* In spring and early summer, White-crowned Sparrows are tireless, even bursting into song under the light of the moon. They are widespread breeders ranging from sea level to mountain thickets.

Birders are not the only ones who attribute words to the songs of birds. Apparently Alaskan miners called the Golden-crowned Sparrow 'Weary Willy' because they thought the bird's descending three-note song, *oh-dear-me*, sounded as tired as they felt.

Golden-crowned Sparrow: *breeding*

Seasonal Occurrence & Local Range: *White-crowned Sparrows are most abundant in summer and during migration. All 'White-crowns' that remain in winter are birds that breed further north. Golden-crowned Sparrows are most abundant during spring and fall migration. They move from low elevations in winter to high elevations in summer.*
Size: *White-crowned: about 19 cm (7.5 in.); Golden-crowned: about 18 cm (7 in.).*

FOX SPARROW

Passerella iliaca

Fox Sparrows are similar to Song Sparrows but larger and darker overall. They are brown above, and their breast is heavily streaked with inverted 'V's; the tail is rusty, and the lower mandible is yellowish.

Fox Sparrow: *adult*

Like other sparrows, and especially their towhee relatives, Fox Sparrows seem to scratch out a living. They scuffle around beneath shrubs and bushes, using a double kicking motion to flip leaves and dig into the moist soil where seeds and insects lay hidden. When male Fox Sparrows pause from their efforts, they belt out their sweet, sliding song that sounds like a bird swinging back and forth on a trapeze.

Fox Sparrows are most common on the coast as winter residents, and they are often spotted in the tangled vegetation and driftwood logs of the seashore.

In summer they will eat as many protein-rich insects as they can get, since regurgitated insects contribute to developing muscle in their growing youngsters. But in winter, when insects are scarce, they carbo-load and eat mostly seeds. Sparrows as a group are omnivorous, despite their short, conical, so-called 'seed-eating' bill shape.

The name Fox Sparrow refers to the rusty red coloration of eastern and northern birds, reminiscent of the coat of a red fox. Here on the coast, however, Fox Sparrows are sooty chocolate in color, and many ornithologists consider them to be a species separate from their eastern cousins.

Seasonal Occurrence & Local Range: *Fox Sparrows breed on the western Olympic Peninsula and islands along the B.C. coast, as well as in the subalpine meadows of the Cascade and Coast ranges and at sea level on western Vancouver Island and northwards.*
Size: *about 19 cm (7.5 in.).*

SONG SPARROW

Melospiza melodia

The Song Sparrow is a small, rusty brown and gray streaked bird, usually with a central, dark breast spot. It pumps its long, rounded tail (long for a sparrow) in flight. Unlike the bill of a Fox Sparrow, that of a Song Sparrow is all dark.

Song Sparrow: *adult*

Although sparrows may appear rather plain at first, they have distinctive markings on their crown, face and breast, and can be easily identified with just a bit of practice.

The Song Sparrow's low-key plumage does not prepare you for its bright song. The performance always begins with three to four sharply repeated notes. One fanciful interpretation of its song is *pres-pres-pres-byteri-eri-erian!;* another, *hip-hip-hip-hooray boys, spring's here!* It is not uncommon to hear a male singing outside of breeding season.

The most common, year-round sparrow of the West Coast, Song Sparrows take up residence in gardens, forests and hedgerows, where they feed on seeds and insects. Each season, pairs of Song Sparrows will raise as many as three or four families. To not waste time, they start as early as April, and the parents divide their duties. The male takes care of the newly fledged young while the female gets started on the next brood.

Seasonal Occurrence & Local Range: *Song Sparrows eke out a living year-round in a variety of habitats, leading some to call them ubiquitous.*
Size*: about 13 cm (5 in.).*

OTHER STREAKY SPARROWS

LINCOLN'S SPARROW
Melospiza lincolnii

SAVANNAH SPARROW
Passerculus sandwichensis

Lincoln's Sparrows resemble small, pale Song Sparrows but with a buffy wash across the thinly streaked breast and a gray stripe above the eye. Savannah Sparrows are light brown, streaky sparrows with yellow in front of the eyes. Their tail is noticeably shorter than that of Song Sparrows and forked instead of rounded.

Savannah Sparrow: *adult*

Lincoln's breed in mountain bogs and soggy meadows, although in modern times they have also taken advantage of clear-cuts. And so, while some songbirds are struggling because of loss of old growth and riparian habitat, Lincoln's Sparrows are on the rise. Local banding studies of West Coast migrants turn up surprisingly large numbers of Lincoln's Sparrows. Yet their reluctance, once they touch down, to leave the protection of scrubby cover makes them very easy to overlook.

The Savannah Sparrow is a summer bird of open fields and meadows. It perches on fence posts to give its thin, lisping, insect-like song, *tea-tea-tea-teeea-today.* Usually this bird hides in the grass, where it gleans insects and grass seeds. Only as a last resort does it flutter into the air, flying off a short ways before disappearing into the grass again as it lands. A patient birdwatcher will wait for a concealed sparrow and make the best of any brief glimpses that the bird allows. Even a quick flash of this species' yellow spot in front of the eye is enough to confirm an identification.

Seasonal Occurrence & Local Range: *Lincoln's Sparrows are most numerous in April and May, and again in September and October. Although a few overwinter along the coast, most carry on to Oregon and points south. Most Savannah Sparrows head to warm southern climes in winter. They tend to avoid snow.*
Size: *Lincoln's: about 15 cm (6 in.); Savannah: about 11 cm (4.5 in.).*

DARK-EYED JUNCO
Junco hyemalis

CHIPPING SPARROW
Spizella passerina

The Dark-eyed Junco is an unusual sparrow with a dark gray hood, and brown flanks and back. The white flashes on the outer edges of the tail are also distinctive. Juvenile birds are streaked like sparrows, but notice the white outer tail feathers, best seen when the bird is in flight. Chipping Sparrows are the same size but have a gray breast, brown-streaked back and a black and white eye stripe below a reddish crown.

Dark-eyed Junco: *male*

With their somber, dark hoods, Dark-eyed Juncos remind some people of plump little executioners, although their habits are much less frightening than that. These ground-feeding sparrows brave winter's worst all along the coast to Alaska. In severe weather they fold their feet under their bodies and fluff out their feathers on the snow like a quilt.

Juncos are faithful feeder visitors with a special affection for millet seed. Feeder watchers can watch their scrappy social dynamics since winter foraging flocks have a definite pecking order. In summer Dark-eyed Juncos nest in wooded areas. The females incubate alone, but both parents feed the young a high protein diet consisting largely of regurgitated insects. The nestlings quickly develop strong legs and can run for their lives, if need be, at a very early age.

Dark-eyed Juncos make smacking and trilling sounds. The trill can be confused with the song of the Chipping Sparrow.

Seasonal Occurrence & Local Range: *Dark-eyed Juncos are widespread year-round with movements in elevation—upward in summer and down in winter. Chipping Sparrows are summer breeders and seem to be declining in numbers.*
Size*: both about 15 cm (6 in.).*

SPOTTED TOWHEE

Pipilo maculatus

Spotted Towhees are slim, black and white birds with fiery red eyes and rusty flanks. Their black wings are flecked with white, and there are white corners on the edge of the tail. Females resemble males but are dark gray rather than black. Juveniles are streaky but with gleaming, red eyes.

Spotted Towhee: *male*

As you sneak up on the source of a loud rustling of leaves, fully expecting an animal of deer-sized proportions, you may be surprised to discover a Spotted Towhee. These ground-feeding sparrows make an amazing amount of noise as they scuffle in search of hiding insects, using a double-footed kick to dig through the leaf litter.

During the breeding season, these normally shy birds perch prominently on shrubs, mewing quizzically, *t'whee?* The male displays by fluffing up and flashing the striking white spots on its wings and tail, and a speck of light in its ruby red eye is an arresting sight indeed. Towhees add color and character to Pacific Northwest gardens and the undergrowth of coastal forests.

These birds were formerly known as the Rufous-sided Towhee, but taxonomists have recently determined that they are a separate species from their eastern relatives. In some ways it is unfortunate that their name wasn't changed to 'Spotted Sparrow' since it is not immediately obvious to the beginner that both towhees and juncos are merely sparrows with unusually attractive coloration.

Seasonal Occurrence & Local Range: *Spotted Towhees are year-round residents in shrubby areas and in forest edges from mid-Vancouver Island and the Mainland south along the coast. Sometimes, in winter, they move down from higher elevations to valley bottoms.*
Size: *about 18 cm (7 in.).*

 CROSSBILLS

RED CROSSBILL
Loxia curvirostra

**WHITE-WINGED
CROSSBILL**
Loxia leucoptera

The Red Crossbill is a medium sized, big-headed, red finch with crossed mandibles. The female is olive-yellow, and immatures are heavily streaked. White-winged Crossbills are similar but have two white wing bars. White-winged males are bright pink rather than red.

Red Crossbill: *male*

A metallic *kip-kip-kip!* call given in undulating flight is the hallmark of Red Crossbills. These red-feathered gypsies wander widely in search of cone crops, nesting when they find bumper crops, regardless of the season.

In the Northwest Coast region, Red Crossbills specialize in fir, spruce and hemlock. Individuals are either right-beaked or left-beaked in opening their cones. They use their curved, crossed bill to pry open the cones, then use their tongue to remove the seed at the base of each cone scale. They do this with amazing rapidity, sending down a rain of cone scales from the treetops.

Recently, ornithologists have discovered that slight differences in bill size and calls may be clues to the presence of as many as eight separate species within what is now called the Red Crossbill. Birders will not be able to separate them, however, and the name Red Crossbill will probably still be used by all but the specialists.

White-winged Crossbills are a bird of the northern boreal forest, where they are spruce cone specialists. They are prone to 'irruptions'—periods of very high population density and dispersal into areas not normally inhabited by this species. Irruptions are triggered by low seed numbers in the northern forests.

Seasonal Occurrence & Local Range: *Red Crossbills range widely but irregularly all along the coasts of Oregon, Washington and B.C. The same is true for White-winged Crossbills but only during irruption years.*
Size: *both about 14 cm (5.5 in.).*

SMALL, STREAKED, RED FINCHES

HOUSE FINCH
Carpodacus mexicanus

PURPLE FINCH
Carpodacus purpureus

COMMON REDPOLL
Carduelis flammea

The male House Finch is streaky with raspberry-colored feathers on the forehead and throat. The tail is square ended. The male Purple Finch is reddish all over and only the back is streaked. The tail is deeply notched. Female Purple Finches are streaked brown with a dark jaw stripe and ear patch, but female House Finches lack strong head markings. Common Redpolls are small, streaky birds wearing a little, red beret and a black goatee.

male

female

House Finch: *adults*

Many people have a hard time sorting out finches but, nevertheless, are delighted by their raspberry color and sweet songs. The House Finch, the most common of the group in suburbia, is a year-round resident in southern British Columbia, Washington and Oregon. The Purple Finch, on the other hand, is a resident of mixed forests and parks.

Both finches are common feeder visitors. House Finch songs are best distinguished by harsh *dzeee* notes; Purple Finch songs are more or less pure warblings. House Finch calls sound like *weet!*, but Purple Finches call with a dry *pik!*.

The House Finch was once a popular cage bird, and as a result, it has been accidentally introduced into eastern North America, where its range is steadily expanding. Some birdwatchers welcome the colorful invader to their feeders, but others lament the disruption of native bird faunas. Here on the West Coast, the House Finch is a native species.

Be careful, as well, not to mistake a Common Redpoll for one of this group. The smaller redpolls are uncommon winter visitors only, and they are actually more closely related to Pine Siskins and American Goldfinches.

female

male

Purple Finch: *adults*

Seasonal Occurrence & Local Range: *House Finches are year-round residents from the southern B.C. coast southwards. Purple Finches extend further north, especially in summer. Redpolls are occasional visitors to our area.*
Size: *House and Purple Finch about 15 cm (6 in.), Redpoll: about 12 cm (5 in.)*

PINE SISKIN 🌲 ⛰

Carduelis pinus

The Pine Siskin is a small, heavily streaked finch with a notched tail. It has yellow wing bars and yellow feathers at the base of the tail.

Pine Siskin: *adult*

Siskins keep up a constant chatter punctuated by a buzzy, questioning *szeeee?* This sound is your clue to look way up and spot a flock of these lively, little finches clinging to cones on the tops of alder and birch, and plucking seeds with their sharply pointed bills.

Pine Siskins swarm through the skies, alighting in treetops. Feeding furiously, they move down the tree, arriving and departing with what seems like a common consciousness. Traveling in winter flocks of 50 to 1000, they pick clean an area and then depart for a new location.

Siskins will readily come to feeders, especially where their favorite thistle (niger) seeds are on the menu. Jostling around the feeder, they are feisty, asserting their dominance by raising their wings straight above their head and flaring their tail. In spring the large, winter flocks break up, as couples pair off for nesting. Yet these social birds form small feeding groups even during the breeding season.

Seasonal Occurrence & Local Range: *Pine Siskins are year-round residents all along the coast.*
Size: *about 11 cm (4.5 in.).*

AMERICAN GOLDFINCH

Carduelis tristis

The breeding male American Goldfinch is a small, yellow finch with a black forehead and wings, and a notched tail. With its bright color pattern, it is unmistakable. The female is duller but is still an attractive yellow 'wild canary' in its own right. In winter both sexes are tan colored instead of yellow. Typical of finches, they have an undulating, roller coaster flight style.

American Goldfinch: *breeding male*

In summer American Goldfinches descend in golden, gleaming flocks wherever there are seed-laden thistles or dandelions. Ironically, these oft-cursed weeds are the center of life for these beautiful birds. Goldfinches delay their nesting to coincide with the season's new crop and then build tightly woven nests lined with thistle down.

Thistle seeds are the preferred food for young and adults alike. Goldfinches fill their crops with the seeds and return to their nest, where they regurgitate the partially digested seeds into their babies' mouths. Most birds typically add a little insect protein to their nestlings' diet, but American Goldfinches seem to make do almost exclusively with thistles.

The state bird of Washington, American Goldfinches migrate in large flocks as far south as Mexico and return again in May, heralding their arrival with their exuberant flight call, *po-ta-to chip!* When perched on their territory, males give forth with a more musical song as well.

Seasonal Occurrence & Local Range: *In summer the American Goldfinch's range extends to the north end of Vancouver Island and to the same extent on the B.C. Mainland. In winter these birds remain only in southern B.C., including the southern tip of Vancouver Island, and south through the Pacific states.*
Size: *about 13 cm (5 in.).*

GRAY-CROWNED ROSY-FINCH

Leucosticte tephrocotis

female

male

The Gray-crowned Rosy-Finch is a sparrow-sized, brown bird splashed with pink on its back, breast and wings. A gray crown goes from eye to eye. Females are duller and the gray crown is less extensive. These finches walk instead of hop.

Gray-crowned Rosy-Finch: *adults*

In the high alpine, where snow lingers late, a smattering of small, dark finches swoops in to feed on wind-blown seeds and insects on the edge of snowfields. These birds are likely to be hardy Gray-crowned Rosy-Finches.

Despite their seemingly frivolous colors and small size, these birds can cope with harsh environments. Their long, pointed wings are an adaptation to flying in their wind-swept habitat, and they walk instead of hop, which may help prevent them from being picked up and tossed by the wind. In summer these rosy-finches develop cheek pouches that enable them to carry back large loads of food to their nesting chicks, which are tucked into a crevice in the rocks for protection.

In times of extreme winter conditions and heavy snowfalls, Gray-crowned Rosy-Finches may briefly visit lower elevations in search of food, favoring shorelines and gravelly areas. Despite their unusual looks and habitat, these rosy-finches sound very much like House Sparrows.

Seasonal Occurrence & Local Range: *In summer Gray-crowned Rosy-Finches are found in B.C. and Washington, usually above 2000 meters (6500 feet), in the alpine. In winter they may drop in elevation.*
Size: *about 14 cm (5.5 in.).*

SNOW BIRDS

SNOW BUNTING
Plectrophenax nivalis

LAPLAND LONGSPUR
Calcarius lapponicus

In winter Snow Buntings are mottled white and brown. No other songbird shows as much white in its wings in flight. Lapland Longspurs are almost the same size and shape, but darker, with a rusty collar and all-brown wings.

male

female

Snow Bunting: *non-breeding*

These two species of northern songbird are similar in habit, and both are seen infrequently in our area.

Snow Buntings and Lapland Longspurs are both 'snow birds.' They breed in the northern tundra and winter in southern Canada and the northern United States. Even in winter, they sleep snugly in snowdrifts and feed on seeds exposed by the wind. Only when severe snowfalls bury their food sources do they show up in fields or on shores in B.C. or northern Washington, flying like a swirling cloud of snowflakes.

Snow Buntings are nervous birds, and for this reason they are a joy to watch. The entire flock descends to the ground, feeds for a moment and suddenly lifts off as one, but with no intention of going very far. After a swirl or two, the flock re-alights, only to repeat the performance over and over again. Perhaps this habit comes from the fact that just about every species of bird-eating raptor in the Northwest Coast area will try to catch Snow Buntings (and Lapland Longspurs).

Seasonal Occurrence & Local Range: *Snow Buntings and Lapland Longspurs are strictly winter visitors to open, often gravelly habitats. The West Coast is off their main migration routes, so we rarely see them here. Along the coast, they are almost always seen along the seashore near beaches and jetties.*
Size: *both about 15 cm (6 in.).*

GROSBEAKS

BLACK-HEADED GROSBEAK 🌲
Pheucticus melanocephalus

EVENING GROSBEAK 🌲⛰
Coccothraustes vespertinus

PINE GROSBEAK ⛰
Pinicola enucleator

Male Black-headed Grosbeaks have a stout bill and an orange brown breast that contrasts sharply with their black head, back and wings. Females have a striped head pattern and are buff and brown. Evening Grosbeaks are large finches with a massive, yellow bill, lovely yellow, brown and black plumage, and big white wing patches on black wings and tail. Females are duller. Pine Grosbeaks are large, reddish finches with a short, black, heavy bill. Females are olive-gray.

female

male

Black-headed Grosbeak: *adults*

These three species are grouped together here because they share a large, seed-eating bill, a 'gross beak,' in other words. However, they are not each other's closest relatives—the Black-headed Grosbeak is related to sparrows and the other two species are finches.

In spring small numbers of Black-headed Grosbeaks arrive from Mexico, the males and females looking almost like two different species. It is easy to overlook these birds because they sound similar to American Robins and tend to remain high in the forest canopy.

male

female

Evening Grosbeak: *adults*

Evening Grosbeaks raise their young in forest-shrouded mountains, then coalesce into flocks at the end of the breeding season. They have a loud whistle-like *pteer!* call that helps the flock remain intact as the birds bound through the air, ever on the lookout for new food sources. Birdwatchers often twig onto the new sound in their neighborhood bird soundscape and search the trees for a good look at these colorful birds.

These big, bonny finches touch down at feeders in fall, sometimes staying the entire winter. Despite the Evening Grosbeaks' voracious appetite for sunflower seeds, many folks are happy to keep topping up their feeders in exchange for the honor of watching them. More fleeting glimpses of these birds can be had on snowy highways, where they congregate to feed on road salt.

Pine Grosbeaks are beautiful, 'soft-spoken' birds that feed in small flocks on a varied fare of fruit, seeds and buds. These slow-moving, plump, pink finches of northern reaches and high mountains are the largest of their family.

male

female

Pine Grosbeak: *adults*

Seasonal Occurrence & Local Range: *Black-headed Grosbeaks are uncommon breeders. Evening Grosbeaks appear in May and again in fall and winter. They are most common on the mainland. Pine Grosbeaks are year-round residents in the Coast and Cascade ranges and on the Queen Charlottes.* **Size:** *Black-headed and Evening: about 20 cm (8 in.); Pine: about 25 cm (10 in.).*

HOUSE SPARROW
Passer domesticus

A brown back and hood, stubby conical bill and a black bib on a white breast give the male House Sparrow a handsome, but dirty-faced appearance. The nondescript female wears gray-brown plumage above and plain gray below.

female

male

House Sparrow: *adults*

Although familiar to everyone because of their urban-dwelling ways, House Sparrows are more exotic than they may seem. They are actually weaver finches, with impressive relatives in the Old World that construct huge colonies of hanging, woven nests. Like these relatives, House Sparrows can construct round, dome-shaped nests, but they have come to prefer moving into cracks and crevices in buildings, weaving under cover.

Native to Europe and the British Isles, House Sparrows were first introduced in Brooklyn, New York, to control caterpillars of the linden moth, a pest to city shade trees. The people who brought the House Sparrow here also argued that it was a good-looking bird that would be nice to have around. While House Sparrows do eat many insects, they have found strength in adaptability, eating whatever they find. The linden moth, by the way, is still a pest in New York.

Like little hobos, House Sparrows extended their range by riding the rails. Attracted to railroad cars shipping grain, House Sparrows were sometimes inadvertently shut into cars, then released again far away when the rail car was re-opened. Noisy and aggressive, they take over the nesting sites of other cavity-nesting birds such as swallows and bluebirds.

Seasonal Occurrence & Local Range*: House Sparrows are year-round residents all along the coast wherever there are human habitations. They do not quite reach the northernmost coast of British Columbia, most likely because of the lack of human settlement.*
Size: *about 15 cm (6 in.).*

SUGGESTED READING

Campbell, R.W., et al. 1990. *The Birds of British Columbia*. Vols. 1 & 2. University of British Columbia Press, Vancouver.

Campbell, R.W., et al. 1997. *The Birds of British Columbia*. Vol. 3. University of British Columbia Press, Vancouver.

Ehrlich, P.R., et al. 1988. *The Birder's Handbook*. Fireside, New York.

Farrand, J., ed. 1983. *The Audubon Society Master Guide to Birding*. 3 vols. Alfred A. Knopf, New York.

Gabrielson, I.N., and S.G. Jewett. 1970. *Birds of the Pacific Northwest*. Dover, New York.

Hunn, E.S. 1982. *Birding in Seattle and King County*. Seattle Audubon Society, Seattle.

Jewett, S.G., et al. 1953. *Birds of Washington State*. University of Washington Press, Seattle.

Kaufman, K. 1990. *A Field Guide to Advanced Birding*. Houghton Mifflin Company, Boston.

————. 1996. *Lives of North American Birds*. Houghton Mifflin Company, Boston.

Larrison, E.J. 1981. *Birds of the Pacific Northwest*. University of Idaho Press, Moscow.

Lewis, M.G., and F.A. Sharpe. 1987. *Birding in the San Juan Islands*. The Mountaineers, Seattle.

MacRae, D. 1995. *Birder's Guide to Washington*. Gulf Publishing Company, Houston.

National Geographic Society. 1987. *Field Guide to the Birds of North America*. 2nd ed. National Geographic Society, Washington, D.C.

Peterson, R.T. 1990. *A Field Guide to Western Birds*. 3rd ed. Houghton Mifflin Company, Boston.

Reader's Digest. *Book of North American Birds*. The Reader's Digest Association, Pleasantville, N.Y.

Robbins, C.S., B. Brunn and H.S. Zim. 1966. *Birds of North America*. Rev. ed. Golden Press, New York.

Stokes, D.W. 1979. *A Guide to Bird Behavior, Volume 1*. Little, Brown and Co., Boston and Toronto.

Stokes, D.W, and L.Q. Stokes. 1983. *A Guide to Bird Behavior, Volume 2*. Little, Brown and Company, Boston.

————. 1989. *A Guide to Bird Behavior, Volume 3*. Little, Brown and Company, Boston.

————. 1996. *Stokes Field Guide to Birds: Western Region*. Little, Brown and Company, Boston.

Terres, J.K. 1995. *The Audubon Society Encyclopedia of North American Birds*. Wing Books, New York.

Vancouver Natural History Society. 1993. *A Bird Watching Guide to the Vancouver Area*. Cavendish Books, Vancouver.

Wahl, T.R., and D.R. Paulson. 1991. *A Guide to Bird Finding in Washington*. Rev. ed. T.R. Wahl, Bellingham.

CHECKLIST FOR THE COASTS OF WASHINGTON AND SOUTHERN B.C.
INCLUDING ADJACENT WATERS AND NEARBY ISLANDS

Although this book is intended as a beginner's introduction to the birds of the West Coast, we realize that some readers will desire a sense of completeness. For them, we have compiled the following list of the 435 species of birds we know to have occurred at least once in our area. We apologize in advance if we have missed any records, but we strongly suspect that this list is very nearly complete. This checklist is arranged in 'standard' order, and therefore does not correspond exactly with the order in which we treat the species in the main text. Each species has been coded for season of occurrence and breeding status.

Y= year-round
M= on migration
F= fall only

S = summer
W= winter
B= breeding
V= vagrant

❏ Red-throated Loon .... W
❏ Pacific Loon .... W
❏ Common Loon .... Y, B
❏ Yellow-billed Loon .... W

❏ Pied-billed Grebe .... Y, B
❏ Horned Grebe .... W
❏ Red-necked Grebe .... W
❏ Eared Grebe .... W
❏ Western Grebe .... W
❏ Clark's Grebe V

❏ Short-tailed Albatross V
❏ Black-footed Albatross .... M
❏ Laysan Albatross V
❏ Shy Albatross V

❏ Northern Fulmar .... M
❏ Mottled Petrel V
❏ Murphy's Petrel V
❏ Pink-footed Shearwater .... M, S
❏ Flesh-footed Shearwater .... F, W
❏ Buller's Shearwater .... F, W
❏ Sooty Shearwater .... M
❏ Short-tailed Shearwater .... F, W
❏ Black-vented Shearwater V
❏ Manx Shearwater V

❏ Wilson's Storm-Petrel V
❏ Fork-tailed Storm-Petrel .... S, B
❏ Leach's Storm-Petrel .... S, B

❏ Red-billed Tropicbird V
❏ Blue-footed Booby V

❏ American White Pelican V
❏ Brown Pelican .... S

❏ Double-crested Cormorant ...... Y, B
❏ Brandt's Cormorant .... Y, B
❏ Pelagic Cormorant .... Y, B

❏ Magnificent Frigatebird V

❏ American Bittern .... Y, B
❏ Least Bittern V
❏ Great Blue Heron .... Y, B
❏ Great Egret V
❏ Snowy Egret V
❏ Little Blue Heron V
❏ Cattle Egret V
❏ Green Heron .... Y, B
❏ Black-crowned Night Heron ..... W

❏ White-faced Ibis V

❑ Tundra Swan .... W
❑ Trumpeter Swan .... W
❑ Mute Swan .... Y, B
❑ Greater White-fronted
   Goose .... M, W
❑ Snow Goose .... M, W
❑ Ross' Goose V
❑ Emperor Goose V
❑ Brant .... M, W
❑ Canada Goose .... Y, B
❑ Wood Duck .... Y, B
❑ Green-winged Teal .... Y, B
❑ Baikal Teal V
❑ Falcated Teal V
❑ American Black Duck .... S, B
❑ Mallard .... Y, B
❑ Northern Pintail .... Y, B
❑ Garganey V
❑ Blue-winged Teal .... S, B
❑ Cinnamon Teal .... S, B
❑ Northern Shoveler .... Y, B
❑ Gadwall .... Y, B
❑ American Wigeon .... Y, B
❑ Eurasian Wigeon .... W
❑ Canvasback .... Y
❑ Redhead V
❑ Ring-necked Duck .... Y
❑ Greater Scaup .... Y
❑ Lesser Scaup .... Y
❑ Tufted Duck .... W, V
❑ Common Eider V
❑ King Eider V
❑ Steller's Eider V
❑ Harlequin Duck .... Y, B
❑ Oldsquaw .... M, W
❑ Black Scoter .... W
❑ Surf Scoter .... W
❑ White-winged Scoter .... W
❑ Common Goldeneye .... Y
❑ Barrow's Goldeneye .... Y, B
❑ Bufflehead .... Y
❑ Smew V
❑ Hooded Merganser .... Y, B
❑ Common Merganser .... Y, B
❑ Red-breasted Merganser .... W
❑ Ruddy Duck .... Y, B

❑ Turkey Vulture .... S, B

❑ Osprey .... S, B
❑ White-tailed Kite .... S, B
❑ Bald Eagle .... Y, B
❑ Northern Harrier .... Y, B
❑ Sharp-shinned Hawk .... Y, B
❑ Cooper's Hawk .... Y, B
❑ Northern Goshawk .... Y, B
❑ Red-shouldered Hawk V
❑ Swainson's Hawk V
❑ Red-tailed Hawk .... Y, B
❑ Rough-legged Hawk .... W
❑ Golden Eagle .... Y

❑ American Kestrel .... Y, B
❑ Merlin .... Y, B
❑ Peregrine Falcon .... Y, B
❑ Gyrfalcon .... W
❑ Prairie Falcon V

❑ Ring-necked Pheasant .... Y, B
❑ Spruce Grouse .... Y, B
❑ Blue Grouse .... Y, B
❑ Willow Ptarmigan .... Y, B
❑ Rock Ptarmigan .... Y, B
❑ White-tailed Ptarmigan .... Y, B
❑ Ruffed Grouse .... Y, B
❑ Wild Turkey .... Y, B
❑ California Quail .... Y, B
❑ Mountain Quail .... Y, B

❑ Yellow Rail V
❑ Virginia Rail .... Y, B
❑ Sora .... S, B
❑ Common Moorhen V
❑ American Coot .... Y, B

❑ Sandhill Crane .... Y, B

❑ Black-bellied Plover .... M, W
❑ American Golden-Plover .... M
❑ Pacific Golden-Plover .... M
❑ Snowy Plover .... Y, B
❑ Semipalmated Plover .... S, B
❑ Killdeer .... Y, B
❑ Eurasian Dotterel V

❑ Black Oystercatcher .... Y, B

❑ Black-necked Stilt V

❏ American Avocet V

❏ Greater Yellowlegs .... M, W
❏ Lesser Yellowlegs .... M
❏ Spotted Redshank V
❏ Solitary Sandpiper .... M
❏ Willet V
❏ Wandering Tattler .... M
❏ Gray-tailed Tattler V
❏ Spotted Sandpiper .... Y, B
❏ Terek Sandpiper V
❏ Upland Sandpiper V
❏ Whimbrel .... M
❏ Bristle-thighed Curlew V
❏ Far Eastern Curlew V
❏ Long-billed Curlew V
❏ Hudsonian Godwit V
❏ Bar-tailed Godwit V
❏ Marbled Godwit V
❏ Ruddy Turnstone .... M
❏ Black Turnstone .... M, W
❏ Surfbird .... M, W
❏ Red Knot.................................. M
❏ Sanderling .... M, W
❏ Semipalmated Sandpiper .... M
❏ Western Sandpiper .... M
❏ Rufous-necked Stint V
❏ Little Stint V
❏ Least Sandpiper .... M, B
❏ White-rumped Sandpiper V
❏ Baird's Sandpiper .... M
❏ Pectoral Sandpiper .... M
❏ Sharp-tailed Sandpiper .... F
❏ Rock Sandpiper .... M, W
❏ Dunlin .... M, W
❏ Curlew Sandpiper V
❏ Stilt Sandpiper V
❏ Spoonbill Sandpiper V
❏ Buff-breasted Sandpiper .... F
❏ Ruff V
❏ Short-billed Dowitcher .... M, B
❏ Long-billed Dowitcher .... M, W
❏ Common Snipe .... Y, B
❏ Wilson's Phalarope .... M, B
❏ Red-necked Phalarope .... M
❏ Red Phalarope .... M, W

❏ Pomarine Jaeger .... M
❏ Parasitic Jaeger......................... M

❏ Long-tailed Jaeger .... M
❏ South Polar Skua .... F
❏ Laughing Gull V
❏ Franklin's Gull .... M
❏ Little Gull V
❏ Black-headed Gull V
❏ Bonaparte's Gull .... M, W
❏ Heermann's Gull .... F

❏ Mew Gull .... Y, B
❏ Ring-billed Gull .... Y
❏ California Gull .... Y
❏ Herring Gull .... W
❏ Thayer's Gull .... W
❏ Iceland Gull V
❏ Slaty-backed Gull V
❏ Western Gull .... Y, B
❏ Glaucous-winged Gull .... Y, B
❏ Glaucous-winged/Western
    hybrids .... Y, B
❏ Glaucous Gull .... W
❏ Black-legged Kittiwake .... M, W
❏ Red-legged Kittiwake V
❏ Ross' Gull V
❏ Sabine's Gull .... M
❏ Ivory Gull V
❏ Caspian Tern .... M, S
❏ Elegant Tern V
❏ Common Tern .... M
❏ Arctic Tern .... M
❏ Forster's Tern V
❏ Aleutian Tern V
❏ Black Tern .... S

❏ Common Murre .... Y, B
❏ Thick-billed Murre .... S, B
❏ Pigeon Guillemot .... Y, B
❏ Marbled Murrelet .... Y, B
❏ Kittlitz's Murrelet V
❏ Xantus' Murrelet V
❏ Ancient Murrelet .... Y, B
❏ Cassin's Auklet .... Y, B
❏ Rhinoceros Auklet .... Y, B
❏ Tufted Puffin .... S, B
❏ Horned Puffin .... S B

❏ Rock Dove .... Y, B
❏ Band-tailed Pigeon .... Y, B
❏ White-winged Dove V

228

❏ Mourning Dove .... Y, B

❏ Yellow-billed Cuckoo V

❏ Barn Owl .... Y, B

❏ Western Screech-Owl .... Y, B
❏ Great Horned Owl .... Y, B
❏ Snowy Owl .... W
❏ Northern Hawk Owl V
❏ Northern Pygmy-Owl .... Y, B
❏ Burrowing Owl V
❏ Spotted Owl .... Y, B
❏ Barred Owl .... Y, B
❏ Great Gray Owl V
❏ Long-eared Owl .... Y, B
❏ Short-eared Owl .... Y, B
❏ Northern Saw-whet Owl .... Y, B
❏ Boreal Owl V

❏ Common Nighthawk .... S, B
❏ Common Poorwill V

❏ Black Swift .... S, B
❏ Vaux's Swift .... S, B
❏ White-throated Swift V

❏ Ruby-throated Hummingbird V
❏ Black-chinned Hummingbird V
❏ Anna's Hummingbird .... Y, B
❏ Costa's Hummingbird V
❏ Calliope Hummingbird .... M
❏ Rufous Hummingbird .... S, B

❏ Belted Kingfisher .... Y, B

❏ Lewis' Woodpecker .... Y, B
❏ Red-naped Sapsucker V
❏ Red-breasted Sapsucker .... Y, B
❏ Downy Woodpecker .... Y, B
❏ Hairy Woodpecker .... Y, B
❏ Three-toed Woodpecker .... Y, B
❏ Northern Flicker .... Y, B
❏ Pileated Woodpecker .... Y, B

❏ Olive-sided Flycatcher .... S, B
❏ Western Wood-Pewee .... S, B
❏ Alder Flycatcher V
❏ Willow Flycatcher .... S, B

❏ Least Flycatcher .... M, S
❏ Hammond's Flycatcher .... S, B
❏ Dusky Flycatcher V
❏ Pacific-slope Flycatcher .... S, B
❏ Black Phoebe V
❏ Eastern Phoebe V
❏ Say's Phoebe V
❏ Ash-throated Flycatcher V
❏ Great-crested Flycatcher V
❏ Tropical Kingbird V
❏ Thick-billed Kingbird V
❏ Western Kingbird .... S, M
❏ Eastern Kingbird .... S, B
❏ Scissor-tailed Flycatcher V

❏ Horned Lark .... M, W
❏ Sky Lark .... Y, B

❏ Purple Martin .... S, B
❏ Tree Swallow .... S, B
❏ Violet-green Swallow .... S, B
❏ Northern Rough-winged
    Swallow .... S, B
❏ Bank Swallow .... S, B
❏ Cliff Swallow .... S, B
❏ Barn Swallow .... S, B

❏ Gray Jay .... Y, B
❏ Steller's Jay .... Y, B
❏ Blue Jay V
❏ Western Scrub-Jay .... Y, B
❏ Clark's Nutcracker .... Y, B
❏ Black-billed Magpie V
❏ Northwestern Crow .... Y, B
❏ American Crow .... Y, B
❏ Common Raven .... Y, B

❏ Black-capped Chickadee .... Y, B
❏ Mountain Chickadee .... Y, B
❏ Boreal Chickadee V
❏ Chestnut-backed Chickadee .... Y, B

❏ Bushtit .... Y, B

❏ Red-breasted Nuthatch .... Y, B
❏ White-breasted Nuthatch .... Y, B
❏ Pygmy Nuthatch V

❏ Brown Creeper .... Y, B

❏ Rock Wren .... Y
❏ Bewick's Wren .... Y, B
❏ House Wren .... S, B
❏ Winter Wren .... Y, B
❏ Marsh Wren .... Y, B

❏ American Dipper .... Y, B

❏ Golden-crowned Kinglet .... Y, B
❏ Ruby-crowned Kinglet .... Y, B
❏ Blue-gray Gnatcatcher V
❏ Northern Wheatear V
❏ Western Bluebird .... S, B
❏ Mountain Bluebird .... S, B
❏ Townsend's Solitaire .... Y, B
❏ Veery .... S
❏ Swainson's Thrush .... S, B
❏ Hermit Thrush .... Y, B
❏ Dusky Thrush V
❏ American Robin .... Y, B
❏ Varied Thrush .... Y, B

❏ Gray Catbird .... S, B
❏ Northern Mockingbird .... Y, B
❏ Sage Thrasher V
❏ Brown Thrasher V

❏ Siberian Accentor V

❏ Yellow Wagtail V
❏ White Wagtail V
❏ Black-backed Wagtail V
❏ Red-throated Pipit V
❏ American Pipit .... M, W

❏ Bohemian Waxwing .... Y, B
❏ Cedar Waxwing .... S, B

❏ Northern Shrike .... W
❏ Loggerhead Shrike V

❏ European Starling .... Y, B
❏ Crested Myna .... Y, B

❏ Solitary Vireo .... S, B
❏ Hutton's Vireo .... Y, B
❏ Warbling Vireo .... S, B
❏ Red-eyed Vireo .... S, B

❏ Blue-winged Warbler V
❏ Tennessee Warbler V
❏ Orange-crowned Warbler .... S, B
❏ Nashville Warbler V
❏ Northern Parula V
❏ Yellow Warbler .... S, B
❏ Chestnut-sided Warbler V
❏ Magnolia Warbler V
❏ Cape May Warbler V
❏ Black-throated Blue Warbler V
❏ Yellow-rumped Warbler .... S, B
❏ Black-throated Gray Warbler .. S, B
❏ Townsend's Warbler .... S, B
❏ Hermit Warbler .... S, B
❏ Black-throated Green Warbler V
❏ Blackburnian Warbler V
❏ Palm Warbler V
❏ Back-and-white Warbler V
❏ Blackpoll Warbler V
❏ American Redstart .... S, B
❏ Canada Warbler V
❏ Ovenbird V
❏ Northern Waterthrush .... M
❏ MacGillivray's Warbler .... S, B
❏ Common Yellowthroat .... S, B
❏ Hooded Warbler V
❏ Wilson's Warbler .... S, B
❏ Painted Redstart V
❏ Yellow-breasted Chat V

❏ Western Tanager .... S, B

❏ Rose-breasted Grosbeak V
❏ Black-headed Grosbeak .... S, B
❏ Lazuli Bunting .... S, B
❏ Indigo Bunting V
❏ Dickcissel V

❏ Green-tailed Towhee V
❏ Spotted Towhee .... Y, B
❏ American Tree Sparrow .... W
❏ Chipping Sparrow .... S, B
❏ Clay-colored Sparrow V
❏ Brewer's Sparrow V
❏ Vesper Sparrow V
❏ Lark Sparrow V
❏ Black-throated Sparrow V
❏ Sage Sparrow V
❏ Lark Bunting V

❏ Savannah Sparrow .... Y, B
❏ Baird's Sparrow V
❏ Grasshopper Sparrow V
❏ LeConte's Sparrow V
❏ Nelson's Sharp-tailed Sparrow V
❏ Fox Sparrow .... Y, B
❏ Song Sparrow .... Y, B
❏ Lincoln's Sparrow .... Y, B
❏ Swamp Sparrow V
❏ White-throated Sparrow V
❏ Golden-crowned Sparrow .... Y, B
❏ White-crowned Sparrow .... Y, B
❏ Harris' Sparrow V
❏ Dark-eyed Junco .... Y, B
❏ Lapland Longspur .... W
❏ Smith's Longspur V
❏ Chestnut-collared Longspur V
❏ Snow Bunting .... W
❏ McKay's Bunting V

❏ Bobolink V
❏ Red-winged Blackbird .... Y, B
❏ Western Meadowlark .... Y, B
❏ Yellow-headed Blackbird .... S, B

❏ Rusty Blackbird V
❏ Brewer's Blackbird .... Y, B
❏ Common Grackle V
❏ Brown-headed Cowbird .... Y, B
❏ Orchard Oriole V
❏ Hooded Oriole V
❏ Bullock's Oriole .... S, B

❏ Brambling V
❏ Gray-crowned Rosy-Finch ...... Y, B
❏ Pine Grosbeak .... Y, B
❏ Purple Finch .... Y, B
❏ House Finch .... Y, B
❏ Cassin's Finch V
❏ Red Crossbill .... Y, B
❏ White-winged Crossbill .... Y, B
❏ Common Redpoll .... W
❏ Hoary Redpoll V
❏ Pine Siskin .... Y, B
❏ American Goldfinch .... Y, B
❏ Lesser Goldfinch V
❏ Evening Grosbeak .... Y, B

❏ House Sparrow .... Y, B

INDEX OF COMMON NAMES

Boldface page numbers refer to the primary species accounts.

INDEX OF SCIENTIFIC NAMES

ABOUT THE AUTHORS

Nancy Baron

John Acorn

In 1980 Nancy Baron and John Acorn met as naturalists working for Alberta Provincial Parks. A common passion for experiencing the world of nature led them to rendezvous regularly for what they called 'great bird-watching extravaganzas'—field explorations and discussions on birds, bugs and life.

For both of them, really watching birds is the true joy of birding—a way of connecting with life and experiencing nature intensely. Many years later, they are still at it.

When not leading natural history ecotours, Nancy works as a consultant in science education and communications. The former Director of Education for the Vancouver Aquarium, Nancy has also worked for National Parks, B.C. Parks and the Canadian Wildlife Service as a naturalist. Nancy studied at the University of British Columbia, where she received a B.Sc. in Zoology and an M.A. in Science Education. You can read her 'Field Notes' column in the *Vancouver Sun*.

John grew up in Edmonton, Alberta, a naturalist from age five. Fascinated by life's diversity, he has gone on to become a well-known naturalist and writer. He is the host of the television series *Acorn, The Nature Nut*, as well as the birding show *Twits and Pishers*. John trained at the University of Alberta, where he received a B.Sc. in Zoology and an M.Sc. in Entomology.

PLANTS OF THE PACIFIC NORTHWEST COAST

Features 794 species of plants commonly found along the Pacific coast from Oregon to Alaska. Includes trees, shrubs, wildflowers, aquatic plants, grasses, ferns, mosses and lichens. 1100 color photos, more than 1000 line drawings, descriptions of habitat and range and 794 color maps.

5.5" x 8.5" • 528 pages • color photos throughout • softcover
$26.95 CDN • $19.95 US • ISBN 1-55105-040-4

WETLAND PLANTS OF OREGON & WASHINGTON

A concise and accessible field guide to the plants of the rich wetland ecosystems. Grouped by habitat, it describes wooded wetland, wetland prairie, marshy shore, shrub swamp, and the submerged and floating community. More than 300 species, 300 color photos, 74 line drawings, ID hints and more.

5.5" x 8.5" • 240 pages • color photos throughout • softcover
$24.95 CDN • $19.95 US • ISBN 1-55105-060-9

HIKING THE ANCIENT FORESTS OF BRITISH COLUMBIA AND WASHINGTON

Walk amid the silence of majestic giants that towered above the forest floor centuries before you were born. This book will help you understand the ecology and natural history of the old-growth forests of British Columbia and Washington. Detailed trail information will guide you to some of the last trees of their kind on earth.

5.5" x 8.5" • 192 pages • B&W photos throughout • softcover
$19.95 CDN • $15.95 US • ISBN 1-55105-045-5

BEST HIKES AND WALKS OF SOUTHWESTERN BRITISH COLUMBIA

Slip this book into your daypack and go! Almost eighty spectacular hiking and walking routes within about three hours of Vancouver. Dawn Hanna includes notes on natural history and aboriginal lore along with important hiking information. For a day-long marathon or a lazy amble to sniff the wildflowers, this book will steer you in the right direction.

5.5" x 8.5" • 388 pages • maps and color photos throughout • softcover
$18.95 CDN • $15.95 US • ISBN 1-55105-095-1

BACKROADS OF SOUTHWESTERN BRITISH COLUMBIA

A handy travel guide that can lead you on daytrips through diverse landscapes, heritage sites and cultural events in one of the most beautiful areas on earth. Joan Donaldson-Yarmey's charming, informative commentary is supplemented by maps and photos to help you get the most out of your travels.

5.5" x 8.5" • 192 pages • B&W photos and maps throughout • softcover
$14.95 CDN • $11.95 US • ISBN 1-55105-097-8

LONE PINE PUBLISHING

206, 10426 81 Avenue
Edmonton, AB T6E 1X5
CANADA

202A, 1110 Seymour Street
Vancouver, BC V6B 3N3
CANADA

1901 Raymond Ave. SW, Suite
Renton, WA 98055
USA